A PARENT'S GUIDE TO RAISING BODY-TRUSTING KIDS IN A BODY-SHAMING WORLD

TRUST THE LISTENER

BECCA ALLEN
LPC, NCC, CEDS-C, PMH-C

Trust the Listener

Published by Reaching & Rooted Publishing
www.reachingandrooted.org

Cover design by Mila Pavlovic
Interior design by Panther City Design
Extracted by Cat Lopez
Edited by Naomi Moscoe

ISBN: 978-1-961826-14-4

Printed in United States of America

First Edition: April 2026

Contents

Dedication

To my husband, my constant encourager and number one supporter.

To my babies, may you always know how deeply you are loved.

And to every parent breaking generational cycles, prioritizing connection over control, and building trust in your child's own inner guide.

Acknowledgements

Thank you to my eating disorder community. Without you, I would have never learned what I know today or built the trust in myself to create a practice of my own. The supervision and mentorship I've received over the years have come from some of the most qualified and compassionate professionals in the field, and I hold immense gratitude for the wisdom they have so generously shared with me.

To my clients, thank you for trusting me to walk beside you on your recovery journeys. It is an honor to witness your courage, vulnerability, and growth.

To my editing team, thank you for talking me into writing this book. I never imagined this would be part of my career path, but your belief in me gave me the confidence to share my knowledge, story, and heart with others.

To my family and close friends, if you'd known ahead of time that I was writing this book, I know you would have expressed endless support. I kept this as my secret project while I worked on my own journey of believing in myself and building the strength to ask others to believe in me as well.

And to my husband, thank you for listening to every single worry I had over the year I was writing this. You responded every time with unwavering support and praise. You have always been my number one cheerleader—and always will be.

This book is a testament to the power of listening to ourselves, to each other, and to the stories that shape us.

For Parents Breaking the Cycle

I think one of the hardest truths to face is that our body stories didn't start with us.

We inherited them.

We absorbed them at the dinner table, in dressing rooms, in the small sighs before stepping on a scale, in the way our mothers and grandmothers spoke about their bodies–or didn't.

We learned what was "good" and what was "too much" long before we could ever name it.

The women in my life were fueled by diet culture. It was the air they breathed, the only language they knew.

Everything revolved around shrinking. Losing weight was seen as a sign of control, discipline, and even happiness. The conversations were constant: calories, weight loss plans, new workouts, whose body was smaller, who had gained weight, who "looked great." It was everywhere.

It still is.

Even now, when I'm with family, diet talk surfaces like a reflex. It's how they connect, how they bond, how they express care, through shared dissatisfaction.

And I can see it for what it is: not vanity, but a means of survival. The women before me were trying to belong in a world that told them smaller was safer.

But we can't heal what we don't name.

For me, breaking the generational cycle of dieting and body shame is not about assigning blame. It is about creating space. Space for something new to take root. My mom did not invent diet culture. She was swimming in it, like the rest of us. She did the best she could with the tools she had. And still, I saw her wrestle with food, with rules, with guilt. I saw her make peace with some parts of her body and declare war on others.

Those patterns do not dissolve on their own.

They echo. They settle in deep.

They become the inner voice that narrates our meals, our clothing choices, our mirrors.

But when we start to see those patterns clearly, we have the power to choose differently.

That is what breaking the cycle looks like. It is not a single act, but a thousand small ones.

It's choosing not to comment on your child's body when it

changes.

It's eating dessert because you enjoy it, not because you "earned" it.

It's letting your kids see you rest.

It's saying aloud, "I feel strong."

It's refusing to moralize food or use your body as a measure of worth.

Generational healing starts in the moments that look ordinary. The lunch table. The car ride. The dressing room. The doctor's office.

It happens in how we speak, how we listen, how we model trust.

When I think about my own kids, I picture them growing up in a world that still screams the same messages, but I want them to have a louder internal voice—a grounded one. One that says:

"My body tells me what I need."

"I can trust it."

"I don't have to earn my worth."

That's why I care so deeply about this work. Because when we do the hard, messy, internal work of unlearning our own shame, our kids get to grow up freer. They don't have to spend decades trying to unlearn what we never meant to teach them.

And maybe that's the most loving thing we can do—break the cycle not by shaming the generations before us, but by listening to the wisdom of our own bodies, and teaching the next generation to listen too.

Because the cycle ends when listening begins.

Why This Book Exists

There's a good chance you grew up in a world where body shaming was normalized. Maybe you were praised for shrinking or criticized for growing. Maybe food was something to control. Maybe you were taught to override your hunger cues and to believe your worth lay somewhere on a scale.

Maybe you're a parent now, or trying to break the cycle for yourself. You want to do things differently, but don't know where to start. You know you want your child to trust their body. You want to protect them from the hurtful messages you endured. But you might also realize that this work isn't so easy. While your love and voice are strong, society can be stronger. Diet culture, fatphobia, even well-meaning doctors sneak in with their rules and their fears. They want you to question your child's trust in themselves.

This book is a guide to pushing back.

For parents who are learning as you go, breaking cycles, and rebuilding trust in your bodies, it's not about doing it perfectly, but about doing it consciously, with curiosity, while loosening the control.

This book is not direct medical advice. It's a guide, not a prescription.

Within this book are tools to help you learn what heals this cycle. The truth is, we cannot shield our kids from everything. The goal is to build a strong enough foundation that they know how to question these messages when they come. We can show them how to listen to their bodies, how to respect themselves, and how to trust themselves.

That trust can change everything.

Parenthood, particularly motherhood, does not become our entire identity when we take on the job of raising the younger generation. It is easy for women to lose themselves in motherhood because of how demanding a job it is. You need to ask yourself, "Who am I outside of motherhood?"

The reason I'm making a point of this is that when I ask my clients who are mothers who they are outside of motherhood, a lot of them don't know. All their identities previous to motherhood are now gone, or at least feel significantly diminished in their lives.

PERSONAL IDENTITY WHEEL

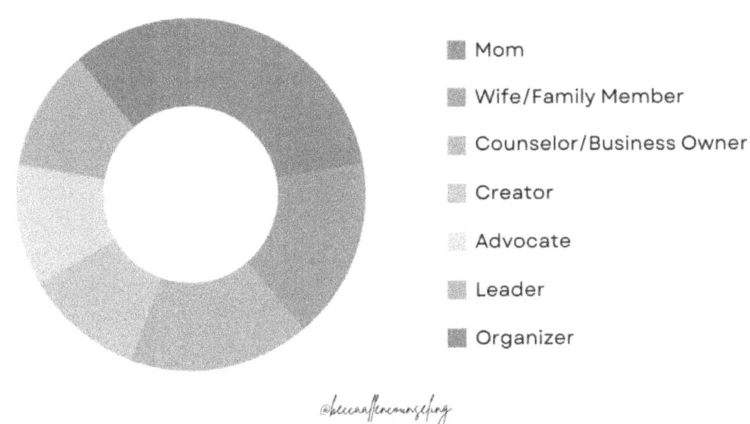

Often, we need to begin by defining who we are before diving into building trust within our bodies. When we think of our identity, we want to think of it in pieces. How much of you is "mother," how much is "wife," how much is "businesswoman," "artist," and so on?

I ask these questions to my clients as an identity exercise to get them thinking about who they are. Within that, we begin to place and repair inherited relationships and stories that no longer serve us.

Patterns around food and control are rarely just about food. Listening to our children begins with learning how to listen to ourselves. And to do that, we must understand who we believe ourselves to be.

Once we recognize our own patterns and their effect on our own relationship with food, we can begin to repair them, and help our children learn what may never have been taught to us–how to trust, respect, and listen to their bodies.

PART I:
FOUNDATIONS OF BODY TRUST

Where Shame Begins, Trust is Lost,
and Listening Often Ceases.

Chapter One

Listening From Birth

Before we can teach our children to listen to their bodies, we have to learn how to listen first.

The first thing listening requires of us is to accept the humbling realization that our children do not grow on our timelines, only their own. Spoiler alert: This never changes.

In the beginning, parenting often feels less like knowing and more like waiting—waiting for signs, for strength, for reassurance that everything will be okay.

When I had my son, Harris, I was an anxious first-time mom, terrified something might happen to him, not least of all because he was born seven weeks early at the start of the pandemic. There was no clear reason why he came early. He just did.

We spent 21 days in the NICU, waiting for him to build the strength to feed on his own and gain enough weight to sustain himself. I remember feeling so completely alone in that hospital. It was COVID and anyone not considered essential wasn't allowed. My husband and I received one paper mask per week which really didn't hold up well with all my crying. We didn't have much support then. We couldn't even be with our son at the same time, even though we lived together and drove to and from the hospital together every day.

It was heartbreaking to watch my baby struggle to stay latched to the bottle day after day. No one really prepares you for the kind of fear that comes with simply trying to keep your child sustained and growing. It was a fear that led me–unsurprisingly–to develop severe postpartum anxiety and depression, especially around feeding.

Every time Harris failed a feeding test, it felt like another step back keeping us stuck in that hospital. I was devastated. Our discharge date kept moving further away. I will never forget the humility of realizing it all: I was an eating disorder specialist. A therapist. Someone who spent years teaching others how to trust their bodies. Yet here I was, with my own child struggling to feed, and there was absolutely nothing I could do but love him, support him, and wait.

I felt like a failure. But it was completely out of my control; there was nothing I could do to build his strength. He was on his own timeline. Not mine. I had to learn to give him time and trust that he would get there when he was ready.

Eventually, he did grow stronger. He started finishing his tiny two-ounce bottles. He started gaining weight. And with every ounce, I felt my anxiety ease just a little. For the first time, I started to believe that he really could listen to his body, and that maybe, just maybe, that would be enough.

Learning Hunger Cues

Almost all of us are all born with the ability to listen to our bodies because we receive cues that signal our needs to our brains. These cues tell us things like "I want milk," "I am uncomfortable," or "I need soothing."

There is this idea that babies do not know what they need when in actuality, they know exactly what they need. They just don't have a voice yet to say, "Mom, I'm hungry." But they do have their ways of signaling their needs.

Parents are encouraged to learn their child's hunger cues as a newborn sooner rather than later in hopes of preventing them from getting overly hungry and then too upset to regulate their eating. Each baby shows their rooting behaviors a bit differently.

Once you learn to recognize your baby's cues, you'll be able to feed when they are first signaling hunger. This is why learning our baby's hunger cues becomes so important. By the time they are kicking and screaming, it means they have exhausted every quieter cue and crying is their last resort to tell us that they are hungry or uncomfortable.

Early hunger cues can include opening and closing their mouth, rooting around as if they are searching for something, moving their tongue, making soft noises, sinking on their hands, or bobbing their head (Best Beginnings, 2023).

These cues are subtle but powerful once you learn how to recognize them. Doulas and lactation consultants are incredible resources. They can teach you to look for small signals, the ones that often go unnoticed when you're overwhelmed.

This kind of support is important because many parents come into the newborn stage believing they are already experts on their child.

If you've had a child before, it's easy to assume you know what the next one will be like. But what happens if they're completely different? Do you adjust? Or do you keep applying your learned experience to a new child, forcing them to fit a pattern that was never meant for them? When parents make decisions based on what they *think* they know about their child, they often dismiss what their child is trying to tell them.

First-time parents can be susceptible to this as well when they over-research during pregnancy and assume everything they studied will match their baby exactly.

They end up pushing those expectations onto a child who hasn't even had the chance yet to show them who they are. That's why I encourage my pregnant clients to do just enough research and resist the urge to over-prepare before the baby arrives.

When you put yourself in the position of "I am the expert," you're more likely to become rigid and struggle to adapt. But if you take the mindset of "I'm going to stay curious and open to what this child tells me," you're far more able to shift as their needs shift.

How Judgment Interferes With Listening

It continually amazes me how much importance gets placed on the size of someone else's body. Babies are no exception.

I remember so clearly the first moment I held my son in my arms. I wasn't prepared for how fragile he would be or what it would feel like to hold someone so light, so soft, so new. I will never forget that feeling. He was my husband's and my only child, so his weight and size was our normal. To us, that was just him.

But from the day Harris was born, I was inundated by comments about how tiny, skinny, and string-bean-like he was. It shocked me how fixated other people were on my son's weight.

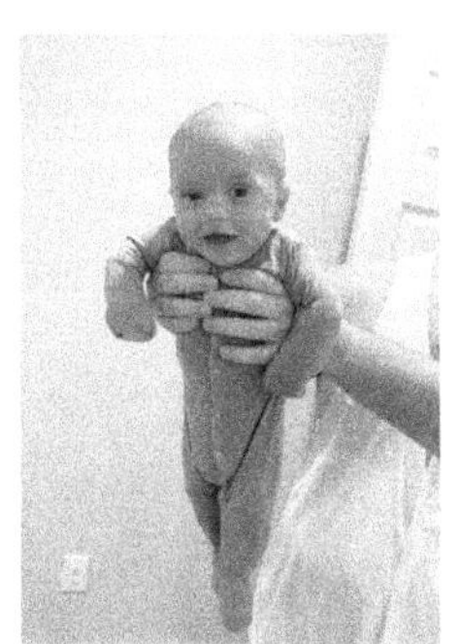

"He's just so little!"

"His legs are so thin!"

"Is he getting enough milk?"

"Is he going to be okay?"

As a new parent, being constantly told that your child is too small, and asked "What's wrong with them?" or "Why don't they eat?" is not supportive in any way. It actually has the opposite effect: You start to wonder if you are doing something wrong as a parent. You begin to think,

"Why is my child not gaining weight as fast as the others?" You start to doubt yourself, your child's signals, and their ability to know what they need.

What I've learned since then is how early people begin fixating on a child's size and how bizarre that fixation is, when you really step back and think about it. We even put a baby's weight and length on birth announcements, like it's the most important part of their identity. Why? Why is that the very first thing we share?

We don't simply announce, "Harris was born at 12:02 p.m., happy and healthy to a loving Mom and Dad." Instead, we say, "Harris was born at 12:02 p.m., four pounds three ounces, 20 inches long." And as soon as those birth announcements go out, the judgments and comments start rolling in.

As adults, we don't typically introduce ourselves by saying, "Hi, I'm 5'5" and weigh 163 pounds." (At least I hope not.) So why do we do this with babies? Why are we judging a human being's weight right at birth?

Our society is deeply obsessed with weight and numbers. When babies weigh more than average, people say things like, "Wow, they're huge!" or "Oh my gosh, what did you eat while pregnant?"

When babies weigh less than average, it flips to concern and judgment, the kind of comments I heard with Harris. "Are they okay?" "Are you feeding them enough?" "What's wrong with them?"

And really, that information should be between the parents and the pediatrician. Yet we've created a culture where size literally from day one invites unsolicited opinions and assumptions. People talk about children's weight as if it's casual small talk.

This fixation on size and weight truly begins at birth.

When I had my second child, I left her weight off the announcement on purpose. It didn't need to be shared. No one said anyhing—at least not to my face. But it made me reflect on how often we share these deeply personal details without thinking, and how quickly it opens the door to stigma or judgment from the very beginning of a child's life.

Their judgment and expectations interfere with your ability to listen.

Too big, too small, too much, not enough: it's this constant stream of evaluation. It's no wonder so many people grow up with complicated, painful relationships with their bodies.

The Obsession With Numbers

As parents, we're encouraged to look outward for confirmation and reassurance that everything is progressing as it should. Percentiles, averages, ounces consumed...monitoring these numbers can be helpful, but they can never become the primary way we understand our children.

What most people don't realize until they have a baby is how much measuring becomes a part of their lives: Every ounce, every pump, every feed. The constant tracking can easily turn into anxiety: *Why didn't they finish the bottle? They usually drink this much. What changed? Is something wrong?*

Growth spurts add to this stress. Babies will drink more for a few days, then less in the days after that. But instead of viewing this as normal fluctuation, parents think something must be wrong.

The measurement lines on baby bottles, the apps that log every time your child feeds, and the scales to measure their exact weight are meant to help, but sometimes they do the opposite by raising our parental anxiety.

Part of this is unavoidable. Everything with babies must be measured to some extent. We need their weight to determine medication doses, and we need basic tracking to understand their needs. The issue is that these tools, and the numbers attached to them, can mislead parents into believing something is wrong with their child, when perhaps nothing is wrong at all.

Instead of connecting us to our baby, they connect us to data. We stop tuning in to our child's cues and start focusing on what the numbers say. We are no longer listening to our baby. In doing so, we lose our ability to adapt our responses in ways that fit the situation.

We forget the simple truth that hunger changes from day to day. Some days we're hungrier than usual. Some days we're not hungry at all. That's normal. But the constant tracking makes the variation feel like a problem to be solved, instead of just part of being human.

Breastfed babies will naturally turn away when they are satisfied and full. They slow their sucking, close their mouths, or fall asleep. But for first-time mothers, it can be hard to trust that instinct and if our babies are smaller, parental anxiety that they aren't eating enough gets in the way, so we keep offering more.

With a bottle, the numbers are right in front of you. You can see exactly how many ounces went in and how many didn't. That's when the hyper-focus starts. The anxiety creeps in if the baby doesn't drink as much as usual. That's when parents often re-offer the bottle, hoping their baby will finish "their normal amount."

It's understandable. You're worried. It all stems from love; you just want to make sure your baby is well fed. But this is what our children are learning:

- Don't listen to your body.
- Don't trust that you're full.
- Listen to me—your parent—instead.
- We will tell you when you've had enough.

I want to be clear: I am not anti-bottle. At all. In fact, both my babies were completely bottle fed. The best way to feed your baby is the way that works for both of you.

What I *am* against is the fear those tiny ounce markers can create. The way they make us second-guess ourselves, as if a number knows our baby better than we do.

Some level of anxiety is normal, but some people are naturally threat-sensitive and become hyper-aware of every feed. They are constantly doing the mental math of how much their baby has taken in and how much they have not, and the numbers themselves intensify the worry.

For example, say your baby has had six ounces at every feed last week, then today, for the third feed in a row, they only take three ounces. Immediately, you start thinking the worst. *What's wrong? Are they sick? Should you re-offer the bottle? Are they going to lose weight?*

In reality, last week might have just been a growth spurt, and this week they are simply leveling out. But that's not where our minds go. I can't help but wonder how different things would feel if we did not fixate so much on the number of ounces they took previously and instead listened to what our child is telling us they need *now*.

Letting children tell us when they are hungry or full is far more intuitive than treating numbers like the final authority.

Parents generally understand that every child has different nutritional needs: Some babies take much more than average from the very beginning, and others take much less. We can accept that variability between different children. What we struggle with is variability with our individual children. When there's a sudden dip or a spike in intake, even if it's normal, we panic because it breaks the pattern we've attached ourselves to.

This is why so many moms obsessively compare numbers with each other and in doing so, they unintentionally create more anxiety. One baby might naturally be a bigger eater, while another simply isn't. But the mom with the "smaller" or "bigger" eater starts to worry she's feeding her baby too little or too much, when really, her child just has different feeding needs.

It's all part of our cultural obsession with tracking everything about our children and how it's reinforced everywhere. Parents download apps that record every poo, pee, ounce, and pump. Daycares and nannies track intake, too. The message becomes constant: Monitor everything. It's no wonder parents feel overwhelmed.

But imagine if we tracked only what actually mattered: That they ate, that they peed, that they pooped. That's enough information to tell us the basics without all the metrics. Wet diapers show hydration. Hunger cues show hunger and that they are ready to eat. The rest is often just noise that brings anxiety instead of clarity.

Key Takeaways

Before we can teach our children to trust their bodies, we first have to learn how to listen. This requires us to accept that our children do not grow on our timelines–only their own. Once you accept this, and learn to listen to your child, you can stop trying to rush, fix, or force things that need to happen in your child's own time. Your role is to support your child, not override their own internal cues.

Babies are born knowing what they need. They communicate hunger, fullness, and comfort, just not with words. Early cues are quiet, but they are clear and present once we learn to listen and recognize them. It's important that we learn our child's cues early so we can meet their needs before they become urgent and cause distress.

Part of listening entails letting go of the view of ourselves as "the expert" on our child based on previous experience with another child or over-research during pregnancy. What worked before, may not work now, and our child may not exactly match everything we studied. Rigid expectations block our ability to respond to what's real. When we impose expectations on our child, we are not listening.

External judgment and expectations also interfere with your ability to listen. Our society is obsessed with numbers and body size, and judgment begins at birth. Other people's unsolicited opinions on our child's size and weight, even when well-intended, create doubt in ourselves as parents, and doubt in our child's internal cues and their ability to communicate them.

A focus on ounces, percentiles, and tracking apps can disconnect us from our child's cues and lead us to parent according to data (that is not even based on our child) instead of the individual human in front of us. When we override their fullness cues, push "just one more ounce," and chase consistency in things like growth and appetite, which naturally fluctuate, we teach our children to distrust their bodies.

Letting children tell us when they are hungry or full is far more intuitive than treating numbers like the final authority.

Chapter Two

Re-Evaluating Our Rules Around Food and Eating

It's easy for parents to draw connections between food and health outcomes, especially when they're trying to do what they believe is best for their children. But many of these connections are based on anecdotes, I-am-the-expert logic, or family lore.

And yet parents will often restrict or withhold a food their children enjoy in order to uphold food rules they have inherited, or adopted as part of a popular health trend that are not based on evidence, and sometimes have even been disproven.

Take the old adage about avoiding dairy when you're sick. People say it has something to do with mucus development, but this has been long since debunked. The creamy texture of many dairy products just makes you more aware of the mucus that's already there.

If that feeling doesn't bother your kid, and they want milk while they're sick, let them have it.

Milk is actually a perfect example of a food children enjoy that is often unnecessarily restricted. Many people are surprised to discover how much milk that my daughter, Olivia, drinks. What can I say–she freaking loves milk. It soothes her, it satisfies her, it fills her cup–literally. She even recently started saying, "I need my milky." (It's adorable.)

It's not that Olivia *really* drinks that much milk. People are surprised because of their perception of milk as something to be restricted. There's a lot of hate on milk in the parent community at the moment, despite it being an excellent source of vitamin D and calcium (Niewijk, 2025).

Many parents are concerned about their kids drinking their calories, and believe that if their kids drink too much milk, it's going to ruin their appetite or cause weight gain. So often, I hear from the clients about their deep fear of their children being fat. Sometimes it's because they were fat children themselves and remember the pain of being teased or excluded. Sometimes it's because they're currently living in a larger body and want to spare their child from the same judgment or bullying they've endured.

And I understand that fear. I really do. It's valid. It comes from a place of love and protection. But the way some parents try to protect their children—by restricting foods they've labeled as "bad," "unhealthy," or "too high in calories"--can actually cause far more harm than the thing they're trying to prevent.

When we teach children to fear food or their own appetites,

when we imply that certain bodies are unacceptable, we're not protecting them. We're teaching them not to trust themselves and lay the foundation for body shame and disordered eating.

I have a friend who sees milk as "wasted calories," so she limits it out of concern for her children's weight—even though they really enjoy it. At one point she shared that when she stopped letting her kids drink milk, their allergies seemed to go away.

None of the evidence-based research I've reviewed shows a clear link between milk consumption and other allergies resolving. My sense is that something else changed and the improvement in allergies happened to coincide with removing milk.

Juice has its share of critics, too. You'll often hear statements like, "Children don't need juice" or "juice is wasted calories." But if it's 100% juice, it comes from fruit, so it's worth questioning why it's labeled as a problem. Juice can be fun, enjoyable, and convenient. Some people focus heavily on the sugar content, but if that same fruit were eaten in its whole form, it would contain a similar amount of sugar, and for most kids, it's not the entirety of their diet. Milk is just milk, and juice is just juice.

I had a friend growing up that followed many wives' tales about food, including milk. It's worth noting she came from a culture that traditionally does not cook with much dairy.

She would also tell me things like, "If you eat cake straight out of the oven, it gives you diarrhea." My entire family still giggles about that to this day.

This theory has been tested in my own kitchen, and I can confidently say it is not accurate. But people tend to hold on to these kinds of beliefs because it's what they were taught, similar to the idea that you have to wait 30 minutes after eating before getting in the pool. These messages get passed down and followed as if they are absolute truths, even when they aren't grounded in evidence.

There are so many old wives' tales when it comes to what you should feed your child and not feed your child. So much of what is fun for a child has been ruined based on ideas and fears that are not based on facts.

It's hard not to let ingrained food rules creep into our approach to feeding our children. It's not that they are always baseless. Yes, sure, if someone drank too much milk at once they might be too full for their next meal. But that is also okay. There are ways around that.

If you find your child's milk intake getting in the way of usual meal intake, think about other ways you can have both the meal and the milk. Play around with different amounts or times of milk and meals. Remember, you don't need an all or nothing mentality when it comes to milk or any other foods.

Instead of controlling our children's bodies or restricting their food, what if we focused on building trust? Trust in their bodies. Trust in their hunger. Trust in their ability to grow into the bodies that are right for them. This shift doesn't mean we abandon structure–it means we offer that structure with compassion.

Your child isn't born knowing what a "balanced meal" looks like, but balance can be taught. Body awareness is what allows it to stick.

When children hear food being judged, they begin to wonder how that applies to them. They might start thinking, *Does that mean I shouldn't eat that either? What if I wanted to? Should I even ask?*

These moments happen quickly, and when statements about food are made casually in front of children, those messages can be internalized before anyone even realizes it has happened.

I would never suggest to my family or my clients that they cannot have *any* rules around food. Some boundaries are necessary. If there is something I am not willing for my children to have, I will not have it in front of them, the exception being "adult" things like alcohol or caffeine. In those cases, I am transparent with them and simply say, "This has caffeine, so it's not something for kids."

If my children ever ask, "Why do you get that and I don't?" I feel confident explaining my reasoning. My decisions are not coming from a diet culture mindset, they are about safety and age appropriateness.

We provide a variety of foods, model a peaceful relationship with eating, and allow children to listen to their own cues without shame or pressure. To do that, we have to let go of the fear that food will harm them and replace it with the belief that a trusting relationship with food and body will protect them far more than any restriction ever could. Because when children feel safe in their bodies, they are more resilient, more self-assured, and better equipped to handle the world's noise.

When Parents Override Their Children's Internal Cues

Most children are born with the ability to listen to their bodies. This ability is innate. It doesn't need to be taught, only protected. But for many children, those signals get overridden early on—most often by the adults who love them the most.

Parents often think they know better than their child about what they should or should not eat. They pick up this idea from varying sources, such as other parents, grandparents, their doctor, and even social media. At the end of the day, however, what parents think is better might not always be what is truly best for the child.

A child knows their body instinctively. Yet fullness in particular is overlooked tremendously by parents. One of the most common examples of this is what Jenn Baswick calls the "clean plate club" (2024): A child *must* clean their plate before they can leave the table or have dessert. This is a forced rule, often passed down from their own parents.

When people grow up hearing, "You have to eat everything on your plate," they often go on to teach that to their kids. It might be a matter of social etiquette in some families, a show of respect for whoever provided the food; or it might be part of a taboo (usually related to scarcity trauma) around what is seen as "wasting food"--usually accompanied by a liberal dose of guilt because, "Children in Africa are starving."

Whatever the reasoning, this rule makes it difficult for children to tune into their body's fullness cues. When they finish all the food on their plate even though they've had enough and don't want anymore, they're overriding their body's natural mechanisms.

If a child says, "Oh, I'm full" after only three bites, a parent's natural reaction might be, "No, you aren't. How could you possibly be full? You haven't had your entire meal." Or maybe, "Okay, but I need you to take three more full bites of chicken before you can be done."

But what they are unintentionally telling the child is, "You don't get to be full. You don't get to stop eating when your body tells you to stop."

The same applies to hunger cues. Our society's fixation on weight and many rules about when, how much, and how often we are "supposed to" eat lead many parents to override their children's hunger cues in an effort to curb or "train" their appetites, regulate their food intake, or both.

When a child announces "I'm hungry" 30 minutes before dinner, or at random times during the day, or (most popularly) the minute they get home from a restaurant, most parents will say something like, "No, you're not," "It's not time to eat right now" (as opposed to simply not having food available), or very commonly "It's too close to dinner, you'll ruin your appetite.

The message to the child then becomes, "You can't trust yourself," "What your body is telling you is wrong," or "Hunger is something to ignore."

But when a child waits to eat, they're often so hungry they stuff themselves and override their own fullness clues or more likely, fail to even notice them because they're eating so fast. Now both cues are being overridden, and the child's trust in their body is further eroded.

If we listen to our children when they say they've had enough, and teach them to trust their fullness cues, then we can also trust in their hunger cues, because we know they will stop eating when they've had enough, and won't feel the need to over-eat because they know they'll be allowed to eat more later.

It's important to remember that pretty much the only consistent thing about children's appetites is that they're all over the place. Kids are constantly growing, but some days they just don't need as much food. They might have been less active that day, or are simply not feeling hungry. Other days they're just feeling hungrier or need some extra energy.

Just as parents struggle with variability in appetite with their individual children as infants, parents usually expect their child to eat the same amount of the same kind of food, around the same time, every day. But this isn't normal or realistic.

Parents can't accurately determine if their kids are hungry based simply on what they, the parent, thinks they need. Only their child can determine how much food feels like enough for them on that day.

Respecting Children's Preferences

When I teach people how to reconnect with their bodies, one of the first things I emphasize is that it is okay to have preferences. You are allowed to dislike certain foods. That is normal, and it should be supported by parents.

Respecting children's preferences is a crucial part of building long-term healthy eating habits. Children are more likely to eat foods they enjoy, and allowing them to have a say in what they eat and follow their inclinations promotes autonomy and helps them develop responsibility for their own food choices.

Not least of all, respecting a child's food preferences helps reduce conflict and mealtime stress, making meals more pleasant for everybody. The benefits of which, I think all parents would agree, cannot be overestimated.

I want my kids to feel confident choosing what they want to eat, so I let them pick their own meals, especially when we are out in public. Sometimes that means they only eat two bites of what they ordered, and other times they eat the entire meal they chose.

If a child tries something and doesn't like it, that's okay. Not every food will be a favorite, or even liked. Now, if you go out to dinner 17 times in a row, and every time they order something, take one bite, hate it, and ask for something new, then maybe it's time to talk about food waste. But honestly, that situation is pretty rare.

When I look back at my own childhood, I sometimes wonder what it would have been like if I had been given the opportunity to have preferences around food. Dinner was simply what was served, and you were expected to eat it. Preferences weren't really part of the conversation. I vividly remember the meals my dad would make, my sister and I would quietly swap the foods we didn't want or like to each other under the table, or spit things out into our napkins, just trying to navigate what felt manageable to eat.

I want to advocate for something simple: it's okay not to like things. It's okay for food to occasionally be wasted. I would much rather my child develop a confident, curious relationship with food—even if that means wasting a little food, money, or time—than feel pressured or forced to like something.

Trying something new should come with the freedom to dislike it. There shouldn't be punishment attached to that.

We all have different preferences. And honestly, this goes far beyond food. Imagine what it would look like if children were allowed to have preferences across other parts of their lives too—what they wear, how they style their hair, or whether they like a particular sport.

Of course, every family will have different rules and guidelines. At the same time, it's okay if a child realizes something isn't for them. Not every kid likes or wants the same things, and that's perfectly fine.

Sometimes it takes someone besides ourselves, their parents, to encourage children to move beyond their existing preferences and into experimentation.

When kids are exposed to new foods in an environment like school, it opens the door to trying things they may not have considered eating at home. As someone who works with eating disorders, I have these little moments of pride when my kids come home and tell me about some new food they tried.

When they came home excited one day announcing, "We had grapes at school and they were so fun!" I immediately responded, "Oh, that's great! Let's buy grapes."

I'd been trying to get them to eat grapes for what felt like forever! They had absolutely no interest when I offered them at home, but suddenly, after trying them in a different environment, it became grapes, grapes, grapes.

It was a reminder that sometimes kids just need a different setting, a different level of autonomy, or a different kind of exposure before they are open to something new. And sometimes, it's just not something we can force at home.

Children deserve their parents' full support as they figure out what feels right for them. Giving kids space to discover what they like and don't like helps them build confidence in who they are.

The Impact of Restrictive Food Rules

Parents impose rigid food rules for many reasons, all well-intentioned. They want to help children develop healthy habits, manage their weight, avoid wastefulness, or to foster structure, control, and discipline around meals and eating.

But restrictive food rules can backfire, and almost always do. They interfere with a child's ability to listen to their body, foster negative long-term relationships with food, and increase their risk of developing disordered eating habits.

Other negative impacts of rigid food rules include an increased desire for the restricted food, reduced self-regulation, reduced enjoyment of food, and emotional distress due to guilt, anxiety, and shame when children eat restricted items–even if they have their parents' permission.

Our culture is incredibly good at reinforcing shame, often in ways we don't even notice. Conversations about food quickly turn into rules, restrictions, and judgments instead of simply being about nourishment or enjoying a meal.

I remember being at a family dinner once where one of the children shared that there was a new rule in their house: no more cereal. She was frustrated and upset about it. What struck me was not just the rule itself, but how quickly cereal went from something allowed in the house to something taken away. It shifted from something neutral to something that needed to be tightly controlled.

If someone wants to balance a meal, there are many ways to do that—adding fruit, yogurt, peanut butter, or other foods alongside it. But when a food is removed completely, it sends a very different message, especially to children who are still learning how to relate to food and their bodies.

One former client of mine was already showing concerning patterns around food at 11 years old. Her diet was highly restricted and as a result, food occupied far more mental space for her than it should have at that age. What she was experiencing wasn't a failure of willpower or lack of maturity—it was the predictable outcome of fear-based messages around children's bodies.

At family dinners, she would anxiously ask, "What are we having for an appetizer? What are we eating? Will there be dessert?" If her family was planning a trip, she'd want to know where they would be eating before almost any other detail. Her attention was pulled toward food in a way that reflected deprivation, not curiosity, excitement, or joy.

She was praised for being "more mature than other kids," a label that sounds like a compliment, but in reality quietly asks children to grow up too fast. When children are told they are mature, they learn to override their own needs, hunger, and instincts in order to earn and keep adult approval.

Adding to this, my young client was surrounded by adults who openly fixated on weight, calories, and physical appearance. Her aunt couldn't be in a social setting without commenting on bodies or dieting, and she absorbed these messages. What she should eat, how she should move, what she should and shouldn't do to avoid judgment, became questions she thought about daily. She was even encouraged toward intense exercise, like CrossFit and long-distance running, long before her body or nervous system could handle that level of demand.

Children do not need high-intensity workouts or rigid food rules. They need permission to trust their bodies, to eat without fear, and to move in ways that feel playful and regulating. When we teach children to distrust their hunger and push their bodies before listening to them, we disrupt a wisdom that was already there.

The pressures of a heavily restricted diet can show up in other ways too. I began to notice that sometimes my client reported being extremely hungry, and other times she would report eating in ways that felt chaotic or urgent. This is a very common response to restrictive diets when someone doesn't feel they have consistent access to food. So when food *does* become available, the body doesn't know when the next opportunity will come and goes full ham. No pun intended.

This may look like binge eating, but unlike binge disorders, this behavior isn't about overeating or lack of control—it's about trying to hold onto something enjoyable in an unpredictable world. When kids trust that more food is available, they don't feel the need to over-eat, hoard, or hide it. The urgency softens, and their nervous system can settle. Once the fear is removed, the behavior often loses its intensity.

Seeing these dynamics play out is painful for me because as a therapist, I'm bound by ethical guidelines that do not allow me to step in or intervene in the ways I sometimes wish I could. Those guidelines exist to protect people, but knowing that doesn't make it any easier to sit back and witness.

What breaks my heart most is how familiar it all feels. From what her mother has shared, this struggle has repeated itself across both parents' experiences and the homes they grew up in. It is the inherited belief that worth is conditional, that safety and goodness are found only in being smaller.

"I am only good if I am small" was not a belief my client was born with. It was something she had been taught by the people she trusts the most.

At 11 years old, my client was already struggling with body image. Her self-esteem was low. She had trouble making friends because she didn't really know how to be herself. She hadn't been given the space to figure that out. She was constantly being told what she should eat, what she should wear, how she should talk, and who she should be.

Reinforcing these messages even further, her parents modeled some very extreme dieting behaviors. Both worked hard to maintain smaller versions of themselves that their bodies likely could not sustain long term.

If they thought their children didn't notice, they were in denial—because kids do see it. Children are constantly observing us and absorbing the implicit messages we send about food, bodies, and worth. They see far more than we realize.

When food becomes so tightly controlled, it starts to take up even more space in a child's mind and actually creates the very outcomes it was meant to prevent—preoccupation with food, body image struggles, and unhealthy, disordered eating habits.

We have to remember that food is our first line of comfort as a baby. It is unrealistic to expect that this connection will disappear as children get older. As parents, we can support the understanding that food can, at times, be a source of comfort, while also helping children build other ways to soothe, regulate, and respond to their emotions.

Boundaries & Flexibility Around Food Rules

Parenting rarely works well when there is only one "right" way to do things. It requires flexibility. It is rarely rigid or perfectly consistent. Sometimes we just do what works in the moment.

I have certainly used a lollipop or two as motivation to get my kids up and dressed on a rushed school morning. Sometimes their cooperation matters more than a lollipop being part of breakfast.

We may even exempt a child from a food rule completely because the outcome of *not* enforcing it takes precedence at that stage. For example, my daughter is three years old and still takes a bottle of milk at bedtime.

And yes, I understand that she may develop some tooth decay, or need a palate expander one day. I understand that dental experts generally recommend stopping bottles at bedtime after about 18 months. But what if you have a kid who will literally only sleep with their "milky?"

Well, then you have to adapt. Examine the pros and cons, and make the choice that works best for your child and family in the moment. You need to have a variety of tools rather than relying on a single rigid rule.

One of the most powerful tools we can utilize is offering choices. For example, if your child struggles to perform tasks because they want to do things according to their own timeline, you can ask them, "Do you want to pause your show to go do that, or do you want to watch your show while you're doing it?"

Giving children options allows them to feel some sense of agency while still accomplishing the task that needs to happen.

Flexibility is far more helpful as an approach than strict rules are. As a parent, you have to figure out what works for your family, and sometimes that flexibility will involve things that other people tend to judge, like candy or screen time. These things are not inherently bad. Like anything else in parenting, they can be allowed thoughtfully and intentionally.

There will always be boundaries, but it's okay to let kids enjoy food and enjoy life. If they want ice cream first or cookies for breakfast once in a while, the world isn't going to end. Now, are we going to do that everyday? Of course not. It is no different than letting them stay up past their bedtime occasionally for holidays or special events.

Another common, almost reflexive rule parents will apply to meals is the order in which things get eaten. Our family went to Jason's Deli here in San Antonio recently. If you've ever been there, you know that one of the major draws is the ice cream. The kids were excited and the second we walked in, it was nothing but ice cream, ice cream, ice cream.

Right away though, I heard my husband say, "Not until you eat dinner."

I let it pass in the moment because I never want to create a dynamic where it looks like Mom is correcting Dad in front of the kids, or positioning myself as the "expert." But what happened next was interesting. Harris ate some of his meal, had his ice cream, and then went right back to eating his pasta and meatballs afterwards.

In the end, the same goal was accomplished: Harris ate both his ice cream and his dinner. What difference does it really make what order he ate them in? I don't worry about whether my kids eat dessert first or last because I trust (and have witnessed) that most of the time, they'll still eat their meal.

And even if they don't, it would be okay. It doesn't happen often, and their regular diet is varied enough that a missed dinner won't impact them nutritionally or developmentally.

At times, it does make sense to place limits around food. But we need to be mindful of what messages we are sending. Say a child goes to a birthday party and has a piece of cake, which is expected and perfectly normal. But later at dinner, when dessert is served, their parents say, "You can't have any because you already had cake earlier."

They may not realize it, but this is a form of controlled food restriction. The parents are limiting the child from a certain food not because of hunger or fullness cues, but because the food is being tracked and rationed. Food isn't just food anymore, but becomes something that must be earned, or something that can be taken away.

If your first reaction to that example is, "What's wrong with that?" it means that somewhere along the line, *you* received and internalized the message that food is something to be controlled and restricted. It's difficult not to absorb that message in our society.

The challenge now becomes *not* passing that message on to our kids. Food should never be a punishment. Children need to trust that meals and snacks will always be available, because when that sense of security is missing, it can contribute to anxiety around food and over time, disordered eating behaviors.

Instead of rigid food rules, focus on setting flexible, healthy boundaries.

So if you just had a Sam's order delivered and your kids are excited about all the new snacks, try guiding them to choose one of this snack and one of that snack rather than restricting them to just one, total, or allowing unlimited amounts simply because everything feels new and exciting.

When parents only allow their child to choose *one* snack or *one* dessert because their child has "hit their limit," they are creating an unhealthy boundary. This approach can turn eating into a rule-based experience rather than one guided by internal cues.

The goal is to stay mindful of the messages you're sending. Boundaries should create structure without rigidity—supporting a sense of safety, trust, and attunement. Over time, these experiences shape how children relate to their bodies, their needs, and even their anxiety, so it's less about control and more about building a flexible, responsive environment.

Allowing Space to Learn

If our children are going to grow up with body trust–to know when they're hungry, to recognize when they're full, and have the confidence to respond accordingly–we need to let them lead the way more often at the table.

Of course parents must set *some* limits around food. But there is an important distinction between a limit and a restriction. Limits help provide structure and guidance, while restrictions can create feelings of control and scarcity, potentially leading to food anxiety and disordered eating patterns.

Limits allow children to trust what's happening inside their own body. Restriction inhibits that trust from forming.

As an eating disorder specialist, I work with families to help rebuild body trust every day. And the one guiding principle I always come back to, the only "food rule" I ever ask parents to follow, is: Parents get to choose what goes on the table. Children get to pick what foods they eat and how much they eat of that food.

This simple boundary honors the parent's role as provider and nurturer while respecting the child's autonomy and body wisdom. After all, their bodies are speaking. Let's make sure they know it's safe to listen.

When children are given space to listen to their bodies and make their own choices, they begin to notice things like: "I'm still hungry," "I don't actually want the peanut butter on this," or "I'm starting to feel full."

I have so much pride in my children and their ability to feed themselves and tell me what they need. It is the one area of parenthood where I can confidently say I've done well. The rest is still a work in progress.

By steering clear of heavy restrictions and rigid rules, my husband and I give our children the space to explore food without fear. I don't scare my kids with warnings like, "Don't drink too much of that," or "Don't eat too much of that because something bad will happen." Instead, I let their experiences teach them.

When we give them the space to notice, to feel, and to reflect, they will begin drawing their own conclusions. At the end of the day, I trust that they know what their bodies need.

Fostering a healthy relationship with food helps children develop both food autonomy and body autonomy. As they learn to listen to their bodies, they naturally begin to notice how different foods make them feel.

Trust the Listener is built around the belief that children come into the world with an innate wisdom about their bodies and identities. Hunger, fullness, distress, discomfort, curiosity, and joy are all forms of communication. When those signals are consistently overridden—through food rules, body shame, forced exercise, or the dismissal of identity—the child learns a devastating lesson: "I cannot trust myself. Other people know my body better than I do."

Children do not need to be controlled into health. They need to be listened into safety. When we trust the listener—when we honor the body's signals, the child's identity, and the nervous system's cues—we interrupt generational harm and create the conditions for real healing.

Key Takeaways

As parents, it's difficult not to draw connections between food and health outcomes in our effort to do what we believe is best for our children. However, many of these connections are not evidence-based.

Food rules are often inherited from our families or culture or adopted as part of popular health trends. Because they are so ingrained, or we trust the source, we stop questioning them. But when we label foods, monitor their food intake, insist our child "clean their plate," or impose other rules that force them to override their internal cues, we teach our child to mistrust both food and themselves.

When food becomes so tightly controlled, it starts to take up even more space in a child's mind and actually creates the very outcomes it was meant to prevent. Far from protecting our child, restrictive food rules interfere with their ability to listen to their body, foster negative long-term relationships with food, and increase our child's risk of developing disordered eating habits.

Instead, we need to create healthy boundaries that create structure, not control. These boundaries should be flexible and take our child's preferences into account, give them the space to notice their body's signals, and allow them the autonomy to act on those signals. Parents should decide what goes on the table, but children should be able to choose what foods and how much of them they eat.

Chapter Three

Learning to Listen: Hunger, Fullness, and Satisfaction

How to Recognize Body Cues and Teach Them to Your Children

There is more than one type of feeling that is associated with hunger. Most people assume that hunger primarily manifests with a growling stomach, but there are other cues that signal that our bodies need food.

Physical hunger cues can include light-headedness, dizziness, headaches, low energy, shaky hands due to low blood pressure, dry mouth, even stomach cramps.

There are also mental cues that tell us when we are hungry. These include feeling "hangry," more irritable, or experiencing brain fog. You may even find it more difficult to make decisions.

There are also behavioral cues, like thinking about food or cravings, and mentally planning what to eat next.

You've probably noticed some of these signs in yourself, your child, or someone close to you—when it's a struggle to concentrate, for example, it could be from a lack of food and energy. Or if someone's hands start to shake, that may indicate they are hungry, too.

Satiation vs. Satisfaction

If you're past the point of being hungry, it can be hard to figure out what will actually satiate, or satisfy, you. When this happens, people tend to eat a variety of foods until something finally satisfies us–but it usually doesn't, because we're no longer connecting our brain and our body.

Compare this to being only slightly hungry. At this point, you can think, "Oh, this sounds good for lunch. A turkey sandwich, or maybe something crunchy, or a bowl of soup." When you're only slightly hungry, you're still connected to your body. You are still present. You haven't stepped away from your reality because you're undernourished.

Sometimes I wonder what it would be like if we just focused on nourishing our bodies with nutrients, rather than worrying about whether food is "healthy" or "unhealthy." These types of labels are not helpful.

Everything has a certain amount of nutrients and both quality and quantity of food matter. The body is far more likely to feel satisfied—and make it comfortably to the next meal—when it receives a balance of protein, carbohydrates, and fat.

A meal of chicken, potatoes, and broccoli with butter will sustain me much longer than broccoli alone, broccoli with chicken, or broccoli with potatoes. The same is true for snacks. Crackers paired with fruit and cheese will keep me fuller longer than crackers by themselves. If a perfect balance isn't attainable, aim for at least two of the three macronutrients (protein, carbohydrates, and fat).

When meals include this kind of balance, we stay satisfied longer than we would after eating a croissant or donut alone. Foods like donuts provide quick energy, but without protein or fat (sorry, the oil it was fried in doesn't count), the body burns through that energy rapidly and leaves us hungry again soon after.

And while we're talking about nourishment and balance, it's worth saying plainly: Coffee is *not* a substitute for a meal! It's a drink—and drinks belong in a different category altogether.

The other side of this discussion is satisfaction. Satisfaction refers to the emotional or sensory experience of eating. How much did you enjoy your meal? Was it crunchy enough? Did it taste good? Did it feel enjoyable to eat?

Satisfaction is about fun. You feel content. You are not deprived of anything. You do not find yourself wishing you had something else. It hit the spot. Flavor, texture, spiciness...these are all factors that can affect your level of satisfaction.

Consider the environment as well. Are you eating in a chaotic restaurant or in the quiet comfort of your home? Are you rushed, or eating at your desk while you're working, or are you able to take time to enjoy your meal? Are you connecting to the food, or just eating to fill a void? Satisfaction is ultimately about how fulfilled you feel by the meal you ate.

Of course, not every meal will hit the spot, but we want most of them to. And with a bit of planning, we can make that happen.

If you love crunchy foods, make crunch a priority in your meals and snacks. One of my most common practical recommendations is investing in an air fryer. Many of my eating disorder clients have sensory preference around food and strongly prefer crunchy textures—mushy foods can trigger gagging or feelings of disgust.

Because of this, crunchy foods often become an important gateway to nourishment. I'll sometimes jokingly ask, "Do you not own an air fryer yet?" because having access to reliably crunchy textures can make eating feel safer, more tolerable, and much more satisfying for many people.

Our air fryer is the most used appliance in my house, second only to the washer and dryer (Mom life, am I right?). If you really enjoy something, include it in your meals. If you love Mexican food, there is no reason you cannot enjoy Mexican cuisine every day.

Growing up, we only drank 1% milk. This was my mom's way of getting us the lowest-calorie option. "If they're going to drink all this milk, I will get the lower-fat version."

The thing is, 1% milk is very watery and doesn't have a lot of flavor. When I eventually tried real milk, I thought, "Oh, my God, this is amazing". I probably would have enjoyed it more, and at the same time drank less because each glass would have satisfied me more.

Ironically, the full fat version of foods often keep us more satisfied than the non-fat versions and we end up consuming less. Calorie-wise, we are breaking even, but we are enjoying it much less.

Fullness

Fullness is your body's way of saying, "I have had enough."

After eating, you tend to feel more relaxed. Emotionally, you feel content and feel you've had enough. You do not feel driven to keep eating. You are not hyper-focused on when your next meal or snack will be.

The sensation of fullness feels different for everyone. It can vary from meal to meal or day to day, depending on your activity levels and the type of food you're eating.

Fullness should feel like a gentle pressure in your stomach signaling you are full. You're not getting hunger cues anymore. Your stomach isn't growling. You're not shaking and your mood is stable.

Fullness should be comfortable, a gentle tightness in your stomach. You know you're "too full" when your stomach is distended or you feel like you need to unbutton your pants. You do not want to be so full that it becomes difficult to breathe.

Children are naturally intuitive eaters. They know when they are full. They lose interest in their food and put their fork down. But this happens only if we are listening to them.

As children build more awareness of their bodies, they will be able to tell you their stomach is full. We need to respect their "stop" signals even if we do not agree with them. This goes back to not overriding your child's cues .

Even small infants will pull away from the food when they've had enough. As they get older, they may lose interest and begin playing with their food, even if they are eating their favorite food, or turning their head away, saying "No." Or my personal favorite, signing "all done."

Hunger-Fullness-Satisfaction Breakdown

Hunger-Fullness -Satisfaction Breakdown

Rating Breakdown

0-2: Overly Hungry
3-7: Normal Eating Range
8-10: Over Full

Definitions:

Hunger

- A physical or biological signal from the body indicating the need for nourishment. It can range from gentle cues to intense sensations.
- Examples of Hunger Cues:
  - Stomach growling or emptiness
  - Lightheadedness or shakiness
  - Difficulty concentrating
  - Irritability ("hangry" feeling)

Fullness

- The physical sensation of the stomach being comfortably filled. Fullness signals that your body has had enough food to meet its immediate energy needs.
- Examples of Fullness Cues:
  - Stomach feeling stretched or satisfied
  - No longer feeling physical hunger
  - Slower eating pace or natural stopping point
  - Feeling like one more bite would be "too much"

Satisfaction

- A mental and emotional sense of contentment with the eating experience. Satisfaction considers not just fullness, but taste, texture, temperature, and how well the food met your needs and desires. Examples of Satisfaction
- Cues:
  - Enjoying the taste and texture of the food Feeling
  - pleased or comforted after eating Not craving
  - "something else" immediately after a meal A sense of
  - completion, not just being full

Hunger-Fullness-Satisfaction Scale

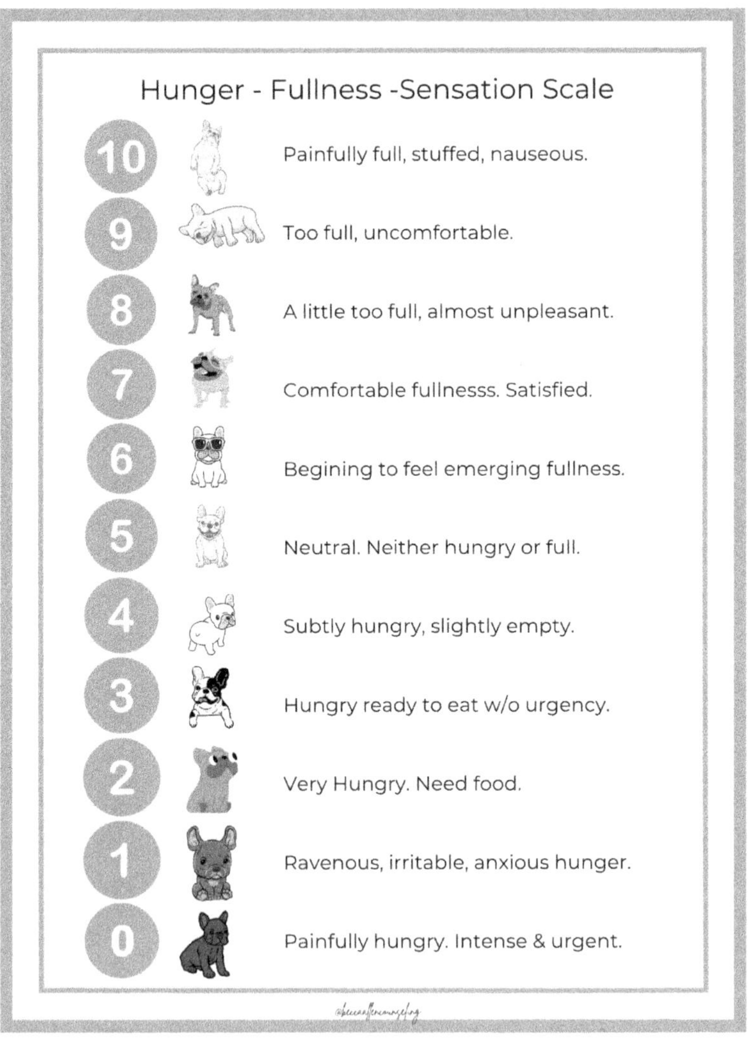

Hunger-Fullness-Satisfaction Chart

Hunger Fullness Satisfaction Chart

Time	Hunger Rating (Before Meal)	Food Eaten	Fullness Rating (After Meal)	Satisfaction Rating (After Meal)	Comments
	0 1 2 3 4 5 6 7 8 9 10		0 1 2 3 4 5 6 7 8 9 10	0 1 2 3 4 5 6 7 8 9 10	
	0 1 2 3 4 5 6 7 8 9 10		0 1 2 3 4 5 6 7 8 9 10	0 1 2 3 4 5 6 7 8 9 10	
	0 1 2 3 4 5 6 7 8 9 10		0 1 2 3 4 5 6 7 8 9 10	0 1 2 3 4 5 6 7 8 9 10	
	0 1 2 3 4 5 6 7 8 9 10		0 1 2 3 4 5 6 7 8 9 10	0 1 2 3 4 5 6 7 8 9 10	
	0 1 2 3 4 5 6 7 8 9 10		0 1 2 3 4 5 6 7 8 9 10	0 1 2 3 4 5 6 7 8 9 10	
	0 1 2 3 4 5 6 7 8 9 10		0 1 2 3 4 5 6 7 8 9 10	0 1 2 3 4 5 6 7 8 9 10	
	0 1 2 3 4 5 6 7 8 9 10		0 1 2 3 4 5 6 7 8 9 10	0 1 2 3 4 5 6 7 8 9 10	
	0 1 2 3 4 5 6 7 8 9 10		0 1 2 3 4 5 6 7 8 9 10	0 1 2 3 4 5 6 7 8 9 10	
	0 1 2 3 4 5 6 7 8 9 10		0 1 2 3 4 5 6 7 8 9 10	0 1 2 3 4 5 6 7 8 9 10	

Scan the QR code below to download these worksheets and more!

Listening and Responding to Hunger Cues

We cannot control hunger. We don't get to choose when it shows up. Because of that, we don't have the luxury of waiting until we feel ravenous before we eat—we have to plan ahead. Hunger cues are important, but they aren't something we can rely on 100% or on demand.

As adults, we are surprisingly good at ignoring our body's signals. We do it all the time. Think about how often someone avoids taking Advil for a headache until they can barely see straight, instead of addressing it when the pain first begins. Or waits to eat until they're starving. We override discomfort until it becomes impossible to ignore—and then we call it an emergency.

For many people, hunger cues are muted or distorted altogether, especially after years of disordered eating. Some only notice physical hunger when they are already hangry—well past the point where the body needed fuel, like a car running on empty. By then, the nervous system is dysregulated and the body has already been set up for struggle.

Learning to listen to your body means noticing signals earlier and responding with care. Whether those cues are about hunger, pain, fatigue, or tension, listening sooner makes a meaningful difference.

When it comes to hunger, this begins with a simple mindfulness practice. Pause and ask yourself: "Am I hungry or satisfied?" "Am I tired or energized?" "Is my body tense or relaxed?"

From there, notice the sensations that arise. Maybe your stomach feels empty or growly. Maybe your energy is low, your head feels light, or your focus is fading. These are all ways the body communicates its needs.

An important part of this process is learning to distinguish between hunger and satisfaction. When you can recognize both, you are better able to respond in ways that support your body—before it has to shout to be heard.

To better understand hunger and fullness signals, I often use the Hunger-Fullness Scale developed by the creators of *Intuitive Eating*, dieticians Evelyn Tribole and Ellyn Satter (Tribole, 2018). The scale runs from 0 to 10 and can help you check in with your body before, during, and after eating.

0 - Starving: You are lightheaded, weak, irritable, nauseous, and you feel the need to eat immediately.
1 - Ravenously hungry: You are feeling shaky and having trouble remembering things. You feel a strong need to eat.
2 - Very hungry: You are thinking about food constantly and feel noticeably low on energy.
3 - Hungry: You are ready to eat. You feel physical signs of hunger but still have time to make a thoughtful food choice.
4 - Beginning to feel hungry: Subtle signs of hunger are starting to show. A great time to plan a meal or snack.
5 - Neutral: You do not feel hungry or full. This is often how you feel in between meals.
6 - Just satisfied: You are starting to feel content, but could eat a little more.
7 - Comfortably full: Hunger is gone. You feel pleasantly satisfied, not overstuffed.

8 - Full: You feel full and are starting to feel heavy. If you continue, it may become uncomfortable.
9 - Uncomfortably full: You feel bloated, sluggish, and overly full.
10 - Stuffed or sick: Painfully full. Nausea or physical discomfort may follow. A strong desire to lie down or compensate may occur.

Normally, you would want to start eating at #**3** and stop eating at #**7**. Staying within this window supports both your physical and emotional well-being. When you fail to pay attention to your hunger and fullness cues, it becomes more difficult to know what you need until the discomfort becomes loud and overwhelming.

You cannot expect your body to function at full capacity if you are not fueling it properly. Just because your body can get by sometimes, doesn't mean it's sustainable to keep pushing past its limits. That's only going to work for so long–and when it stops working, we crash out.

Take morning hunger, for example. It's commonplace in our society to skip breakfast and I often hear clients say, "I'm just not hungry in the morning." And that may be true—not everyone wakes up feeling ravenous. But not feeling hungry doesn't mean your body does not need fuel.

Everyone needs consistent energy to start the day if they want their brain and body to function well. When you skip breakfast, you are essentially asking your body to perform at maximum capacity with an empty tank. Then, when your energy crashes at 10 a.m., it feels confusing or frustrating. In reality, the body is responding exactly as it should.

For most people, "I'm not hungry in the morning" is not the full truth. More often it reflects a long-standing pattern of food restriction, rather than an accurate hunger signal. Sometimes a client will tell me, "I only eat when I'm hungry." But do they really? What on that scale constitutes "hunger" to them? And how are they managing to arrange their life so that as soon as they hit that point of hunger, a satisfying, nutritionally balanced meal becomes immediately available? For most of us, life doesn't pause to wait for perfect hunger cues.

Undoing years of habit can be challenging. Here's a practical suggestion for getting back on the balanced breakfast train: Swap your morning snack and your breakfast–start the day with something small and lower in volume (your snack), then have a balanced breakfast at your regular snack time. It still honors the body, without overwhelming it.

If you want to burn out, surviving on coffee alone is a great way to get there, fast. I've noticed a huge increase in people drinking multiple shots of espresso—sometimes with nothing else. To me, it's like drinking gasoline. I'm more of a latte gal myself and the ratio of milk per coffee has to be just the right color.

I once had a client who insisted she "just preferred" black coffee. But as we talked more, it became clear it wasn't really about preference—it was about the fact that it had zero calories and helped suppress her appetite in the morning.

So I gently challenged her: "Do you actually like black coffee, or is it just what feels safest?"

It happened to be pumpkin spice season, so I asked if she had ever tried a pumpkin spice latte. She said no. I said, "What would it be like to experiment with that this week—just as an exposure? You could even make your own version at home."

The next session, she came back and said, "Oh my God, that was so good."

Of course it was.

So I asked, "Are you going back to black coffee?"

She paused and said she actually wanted to start adding flavored creamer—something that made her coffee more enjoyable, even if it felt a little scary because of the calories.

That's the real work. Not forcing change—but getting curious about what's actually preference, and what's driven by fear.

I often frame these moments as experiments. No rules. No expectations. Just for fun. Use the milk you actually want. Don't make it "skinny." Let taste matter.

This kind of experimentation helps people reconnect with pleasure and preference, two things that dieting actively trains us to ignore. When the goal shifts away from "low-cal" and toward satisfaction, people often realize they have been settling for foods that don't even taste good.

There are so many ways to get crunch, flavor, and nourishment—yet diet culture convinces us to eat dry rice cakes and call it satisfaction. Let's be honest: no one is truly satiated by a plain rice cake. Even rice cake sandwiches require a level of jaw strength no one signed up for. Dieting drains the joy out of food.

Think of it this way: Imagine owning a one-of-a-kind luxury car. You would never put low-quality fuel into it. You would use the best fuel available to protect it, respect it, and keep it running well.

You're one-of-a-kind, too. Your body is not replaceable. It cannot be remade. So why would you fuel it with low-quality "diet" foods, usually the least nourishing options (and most expensive) available?

These patterns are not always chosen–I want to state that clearly. For many people, especially those with eating disorders, disconnection from hunger cues runs deep. These struggles are not solved by simply telling someone (or yourself) to "Eat more" or "Don't eat so much."

That is why *Trust the Listener* is not about willpower. It is about slowly rebuilding safety, permission, and trust so the body's signals can be heard again.

Key Takeaways

Hunger isn't just a growling stomach. There are physical, mental, and behavioral cues. As adults, we are surprisingly good at ignoring our body's signals. But for many people, hunger cues are muted or distorted altogether, especially after years of disordered eating.

Learning to listen to your body means noticing signals earlier and responding with care. When we ignore hunger cues, we are less likely to make food choices that nourish, fill, and satisfy us, because we're no longer connecting our brain and our body.

Fullness should feel comfortable, not stuffed; a gentle "I've had enough." Children know this instinctively. They stop when they're full—if we let them. The moment we override that, we teach them to ignore their own bodies.

Unlike fullness, which is physical, satisfaction is emotional. When meals are not nutritionally balanced and enjoyable, we find ourselves searching for that sense of satiation by eating more or trying a variety of foods until something finally hits the spot.

By learning to distinguish between hunger and satisfaction, we are better able to respond in ways that support our body's needs. We are far more likely to feel satisfied—and make it comfortably to the next meal—when our body receives a balance of protein, carbohydrates, and fat. Not every single meal will contain all three elements, but what matters isn't perfection, it's balance. You cannot expect your body to function at full capacity if you are not fueling it properly.

The Hunger-Fullness Scale developed by dieticians Evelyn Tribole and Ellyn Satter, shared above, can help you better understand hunger and fullness signals, and help you check in with your body before, during, and after eating.

Chapter Four

Rebuilding Trust With Your Body

When you've spent years or even a lifetime being told how, when, and what to eat, it can feel nearly impossible to know what your body is actually asking for.

Maybe you've followed meal plans, food rules, or diets that told you when to eat and when to stop. Maybe hunger was something you were taught to suppress. Maybe fullness was something you were taught to ignore. And satisfaction? That wasn't even part of the conversation.

But you can rebuild trust with your body, with your cues, and with your ability to make decisions rooted in self-care, rather than self-control. It's about moving away from external rules and toward internal wisdom.

The goal isn't to get it perfect. It's to get closer. To get curious. And to give yourself permission to stop outsourcing authority over your body to anyone but you.

Undoing the Effects of Food Restriction

Rebuilding a relationship with food instead of cutting it out is at the foundation of undoing the effects of food rules, restriction, and shame.

Ask yourself the questions:

- Are you an all or nothing kind of person?
- How do you build stability with this food that you love so much instead of getting rid of it?

Spoiler alert: "Getting rid of it" is never going to be the answer. When we under-eat, the body sends a stress signal that increases cortisol (the stress hormone) levels and once food finally becomes available, the reward response becomes even stronger. This in turn increases the potential for binge behavior to occur.

The food we want is everywhere: In our homes, in shops and workplaces, in the media we consume. We have to figure out how to build a stable relationship with these foods instead of cutting them out. If you have anyone in your life that has been in a battle like this with food and against themselves, it is so hard to watch.

There is a deep-seated shame associated with food, and it's tied into the rules and restrictions we have with food. But it is difficult to listen to our bodies and learn how to meet our own needs if we're living under extremely rigid rules.

My own mom has carried food rules for as long as I can remember. Even now, she finds herself restricting herself. It's not something she can just turn off.

We were at Chili's the other night, sharing chips, guacamole, and queso. When my kids got up to go to the bathroom, she looked at me and said, "Okay, that's my last one. I'm not having any more."

I could tell she still wanted them, so I gently said, "You can eat what feels right."

She paused and replied, "Well, then I won't eat my dinner."

Food rules are often rooted in a fear of becoming fat. Everything seems to come back around to "fat." We live in a culture that deems pretty much everything as either Good or Bad. When a food or a food group is labeled a bad thing, none of us want to eat it. We think we are better than eating that food.

Carbs are a perfect example of this, to the point where it almost feels scary or even wrong to eat food staples like bread and pasta. Unfortunately, as a society we tend to follow these ideas pretty blindly and most people don't educate themselves about foods before they decide whether or not to restrict them.

Instead, we often–consciously or otherwise–rely on marketing to determine what foods we buy. Social media influencers, TV personalities, and major brands promise outcomes and position themselves as experts in order to persuade us to buy their foods or drinks, diet programs, or particular food rules.

If we value and trust these sources, and they seem to be trusted by many others, we're less likely to do our due diligence or even ask ourselves, "What is in that? Should I look into it more? Is that really something I want to put in my body?"

Instead we buy things blindly, consume things without much

thought.

Gurus and self-declared experts in the diet and wellness space like to make very clear, very black and white rules around what we can and cannot eat. Carb free, low fat, gluten free, no red meat, lean meats only, nothing processed, whole grains, whole food, whole fruits only...the rules are endless.

So much of our relationship with food has been shaped by opinions, rather than from evidence-based facts.

I am finding time and time again that it takes more energy to sift through the misinformation and find facts than it should. Everyone has a different definition of what "healthy" looks like. There are so many food rules that parents have, that upon further investigation are based on a fear of being fat or gaining weight. Which as we now know is not an arbiter of wellness and good health.

With all of this shoved in our faces, it's no surprise we begin to internalize these rules over time. They become such big parts of our daily lives that we don't even notice them sometimes. We don't think about *why* we take certain things out of our diet, we just do it, and not always just because people tell us to.

We self-impose food rules based on our upbringing, or some ingrained popular wisdom, like thinking we're healthier on a low fat diet. Our cultural fixation on food and bodies is so pervasive that we often follow food rules for social acceptance and non-judgment. We think, "If I eat right, I am less likely to be judged." Or "If I have a smaller body, I'm more likely to be included."

The structure of food rules is comforting and helps us feel in control. Without food rules, how will you control your food intake? How will you know what and how much to eat, how to fuel yourself on your own?

Practical Steps to Healing

Healing from food rules isn't about replacing one set of rules with another, it's about slowly rebuilding trust–trust in the body, trust in hunger and fullness cues, and trust that eating can become an enjoyable, satisfying experience rather than a controlled one.

This process happens in small, repeated moments.

The first step to undoing the effects of food rules is to notice them. Children inherit rules we often never or barely realized we were following. Awareness is the first interruption of the cycle.

The longer you've been carrying your food rules, the more quietly they operate. They say things like: "I shouldn't eat past a certain time," "Dessert has to be earned" (Usually through deprivation or calorie-burning workouts), "It's a waste if I don't finish the whole thing," or the classic "This food is bad."

When those messages come creeping in, ask yourself: "Where did I learn this?" "Is this helping me feel better around food, or more anxious?"

Restriction trains us to override our bodies' signals. Shifting from control to curiosity helps us reconnect with internal cues. So instead of telling your child, "You just ate," or "You've had enough," encourage them to listen to their bodies by asking, "Are you still feeling hungry?" "What's your stomach telling you right now?"

Then follow through by allowing them the autonomy to make their own food choices without shame, pressure, or guilt. Offer a variety of foods and avoid labeling them. Start letting previously restricted foods back in predictably, not as rewards, to reduce food obsession.

Food should never be a reward or a punishment. Connecting food and behavior sends the message that eating is tied to worthiness, rather than their body's needs. Meals and snacks should be predictable and unconditional. Not something they have to earn.

Same goes for you! It's difficult to heal your children from the effects of food rules without healing yourself. If you're skipping meals, openly dieting, or expressing guilt about food, it's going to be a tough sell teaching your kids that food isn't something to be controlled.

While you're at it, stop commenting on other people's bodies as well as your own. Even if it's complimentary, weight and diet talk and centering conversation around other people's appearance can teach children that bodies are something to be judged.

Children learn how to feel about their bodies by listening to how we talk about them.

Finally, be patient with yourself and your child as you undo these food rules. It's a big change and there will be a period of adjustment.

When food restriction lifts, your child (and you) may eat more of previously limited foods. This is not loss of control–it's the body catching up on permission. Don't try to correct this phase; stay steady through it. When access to these foods stays predictable and consistent over time, it will naturally stabilize.

Picky Eating vs ARFID

Picky eating is incredibly common in toddlers. You'll begin to see it around two years old: babies younger than two tend to be more open to a greater variety of foods.

At some point in their preschool years there is a shift and they start becoming picky. They begin to express dislike of certain textures, certain colors of food, or certain flavors, and develop preferences that seem to center around gourmet options like mac and cheese, chicken nuggets, and apples.

It's natural for parents to feel frustrated when their child seems to prefer only a small number of foods, or when something as simple as presentation determines whether they'll eat it. One day a cucumber slice is rejected, but cut it into a star shape and suddenly it's acceptable.

This isn't defiance or manipulation. It's part of how children explore control, novelty, and comfort with food.

But where typical picky eating doesn't interfere with a child's growth, social life, or overall nutrient intake, ARFID does.

While a relatively new diagnosis, ARFID (Avoidant/Restrictive Food Intake Disorder) has been around for a very long time. It is *not* the same as picky eating and gets widely misunderstood.

It can also start at any age and is not a child-only diagnosis. It is not "just a phase."

ARFID involves a serious restriction of foods. This may include avoiding entire food groups, specific textures, flavors, or tastes. Over time, this level of restriction can lead to significant nutritional deficiencies, weight loss, or, in younger children, difficulty meeting expected growth patterns.

Because of these limitations, individuals with ARFID often rely on supplements or nutritional support to help meet their body's needs and prevent further medical complications.

Unlike many other eating disorders, ARFID is not driven by body image concerns. Instead, it is typically related to sensory sensitivities, fear of negative experiences with food, or a lack of interest in eating.

Our brains tend to be drawn to color, and since differently-colored foods often have different nutrients, our bodies benefit from it too. Processed foods, however, often have less variety in color. Many of these foods tend to fall into shades of brown—chicken nuggets, snack bars, french fries, pasta. While these foods can still provide important macronutrients like protein, carbohydrates, and fat, they often contain fewer vitamins and minerals than more colorful foods.

This doesn't mean processed foods are inherently bad. But compared to whole foods—like fruits, vegetables, and other naturally colorful options—they tend to offer fewer nutrients.

Our bodies rely on nutrients to function properly. They help support energy, mood, growth, and overall health. So if we want to increase the nutrients in our diet, one simple place to start is by adding more color to our plates.

Treating AFRID involves a lot of exposure, modeling, practicing, playing with foods, and making eating less of a chore.

ARFID can significantly interfere with daily functioning and social situations that involve food like school lunchtimes, family gatherings, or eating out, which can create a great deal of anxiety and distress. Many individuals worry about how others will perceive the way they eat.

One client of mine recently left for college and shared how anxious she feels about eating in the dining hall with her roommate. She worries about what her roommate might think if she orders pizza, removes the toppings and cheese, and eats only the bread and sauce.

There is no one-size-fits-all presentation of ARFID. Clinicians generally recognize three primary patterns:

1. Sensory-based (sensitivity to taste, texture, smell, or appearance of food)

2. Fear-based (avoidance due to fear of choking, vomiting, or other negative experiences)

3. Lack of interest or low appetite (limited desire to eat or low internal hunger cues)

Sensory-Based ARFID

The first type, sensory-based ARFID, is driven by sensitivities to things like taste, texture, color, appearance, temperature, or even how wet or dry a food feels. Being around certain foods—let alone eating them—can cause significant distress. Because of this, individuals often rely heavily on a small number of "safe foods."

These safe foods are often things like carbohydrates, in part because they tend to be very consistent. For example, a Ritz cracker is almost always going to taste the same every time. In contrast, foods like fruits and vegetables can vary a lot depending on ripeness. Fruit might taste different from one day to the next, or have a different texture depending on how ripe it is.

Take bananas as a simple example. If a banana is overly ripe and mushy, I can't eat it because the texture makes me gag. But if it's yellow and still firm, it's completely fine for me. The difference is that I have plenty of other foods available to me if a banana isn't appealing that day.

For someone with ARFID, however, food options can be extremely limited—they may have as few as five, six, or seven foods they feel safe eating. For this reason, they are often prescribed supplements or other nutritional supports to prevent serious deficiencies and maintain overall health.

Fear-Based ARFID

Fear-based ARFID is driven by the thought, *What if something bad happens?* This fear often develops after a frightening experience related to food—such as choking, vomiting, or having an allergic reaction.

With fear-based ARFID, the fear response becomes so strong that it can take over the body. Sometimes the fear is connected to a real event, like choking or vomiting. Other times, the fear can be triggered simply by the thought of eating a certain food. The person may look at the food and immediately experience a strong reaction of, "I can't do that."

Because of this intense fear, individuals often begin restricting the foods they associate with that experience.

I once worked with a child around seven years old who had choked on a hot dog. His mother was there, and thankfully he was okay. Naturally, he was a little cautious about eating a hot dog again, which made sense.

Unfortunately, when he did try eating a hot dog again, he didn't chew it well and ended up choking a second time. After that second experience, his fear became overwhelming, and he began to avoid solid foods altogether and regressed to consuming only liquids.

At that point, the situation became much more serious. Because of his young age and the sudden drop in his food intake, his growth began to slow. When children are not receiving adequate nutrition during key developmental periods, it can significantly affect their growth. Once those developmental windows close, it can be difficult—sometimes impossible—to fully make up for that lost growth.

Lack of Interest or Low Appetite

The third recognized pattern is a lack of interest in eating or a low appetite. Someone with this type of ARFID often doesn't experience strong hunger cues and has very little interest in food. Eating feels boring to them and brings little to no enjoyment.

Because of this, they frequently forget to eat or only take a few bites here and there throughout the day. Over time, this pattern can significantly impact their overall nutrient intake. When someone is only eating sporadically in small amounts, it becomes very difficult for their body to receive the energy and nutrients it needs.

What stands out about this type of ARFID is how consistent the lack of interest in food tends to be, regardless of what is offered. Even highly appealing foods might not change their response. You could offer ice cream for every meal and their reaction would still be "Meh." For many of these individuals, this pattern has been present for as long as they can remember.

This presentation of ARFID is actually the type I see most often. These are often the people who say things like, "I wish I could just take a pill that gave me all my nutrients, so I wouldn't have to eat."

For them, eating feels less like a pleasure and more like a chore—something they have to do, but would prefer not to.

Treating ARFID

Your doctor may or may not recognize ARFID as an eating disorder. Unfortunately, many medical professionals receive very little training on eating disorders during medical school. Because of that, some doctors may mistake ARFID for simple picky eating and assume a child will eventually grow out of it, which can lead to a lot of invalidation for patients and families.

It is also important to understand that someone can experience more than one presentation of ARFID at the same time. The sensory-based, fear-based, and low-interest types can overlap, and each of them can be equally distressing—especially for children.

On top of that, ARFID can sometimes occur alongside other eating disorders, including anorexia. Eating disorders are not static; they can evolve and shift over time. Someone may begin with one pattern and develop additional symptoms over time, making diagnosis and treatment more complex.

One important distinction to keep in mind is that "picky eating" is not a diagnosis. ARFID goes far beyond typical pickiness. It can significantly impact a person's quality of life, growth, and nutritional health. Treatment is not as simple as someone eating a few meals and being "cured."

ARFID is still widely misunderstood. Many people have never heard of it and those who have, sometimes dismiss it as something minor. A common assumption is that the solution is simply exposure—just keep trying the food over and over until it becomes normal.

While exposure can be part of treatment, it is not that simple. For someone with ARFID, exposure can be extremely distressing. Repeatedly presenting a food like mashed potatoes ten times in a row is unlikely to magically make it feel safe.

Building safety and trust with food is foundational in the treatment of Avoidant/Restrictive Food Intake Disorder. When a child feels safe, they are more willing to explore, try new foods, and listen to their internal cues. However, parents can unintentionally disrupt this process when their own goals, such as wanting their child to eat more or eat a wider variety, take priority over the child's experience. This can show up as pressure, negotiation, or forcing exposure to a food they want their child to eat, and with ARFID, pressure often backfires at mealtimes, increasing resistance and anxiety. A team-based approach with a therapist, dietitian, and medical provider helps ensure care is supportive and individualized, as treatment is not one size fits all and requires flexibility in how change is approached. Progress may look small, but a win is still a win, even if all a child can do is tolerate holding a food in their hand.

There is a documentary called *Not Just a Picky Eater*, available on Amazon Prime, that follows adults who lived for years believing they were simply "picky eaters" before learning about ARFID (Pascarelli, 2023). The film shows how deeply this disorder can affect someone's social life, nutrition, and sense of belonging.

One individual featured in the documentary is a man who wanted to learn how to eat salad. He worked in a corporate environment where dinner salads were often served at events. He knew he probably would never enjoy salad, but he wanted to be able to participate socially without feeling embarrassed. With the help of a dietitian, he worked on calming his body and mind enough to tolerate small amounts of salad so he could feel more comfortable in those situations.

Pizza is another example of a food that can be very distressing. One of my clients who recently left for college had pizza on her list of foods she hoped to eventually feel more comfortable around. But we could not start there—it was far too overwhelming.

Instead, we start by creating a hierarchy of foods, where I have clients rank foods from the most distressing to the least distressing. For this client, pizza was near the top of the list, while something like peanut butter was closer to the bottom. Even the foods at the bottom of the list were distressing, but they were the most manageable place to begin.

It's best to start small. Especially with my adult clients, I give them a lot of autonomy in deciding where they want to begin. If peanut butter feels like the least distressing option, we begin there. That might involve simply looking at the food, smelling it, putting it on a cracker, or exploring different versions of it. Over time, the goal is to gradually integrate the food into their life in a way that feels manageable.

Treatment takes time: it's one of the most challenging aspects of ARFID. Whether someone is working with a provider or making changes on their own, progress tends to be slow. It is not a quick or simple process.

While exposure to foods is one component of treatment, another critical focus is ensuring that the person is not becoming malnourished. Nutrient intake matters, so supplementation is often an important part of care.

We cannot force someone to make food changes before they are ready. Instead, we focus on helping them stay safe while working toward gradual progress. If someone is highly restricted, we look for ways to support their body nutritionally.

For example, if someone were only eating croissants, they might technically survive—but they likely would not feel very well. Croissants provide carbohydrates, but they lack protein. So we ask: "What is another way to get protein that feels more manageable?"

Protein is often one of the hardest nutrients for individuals with ARFID to obtain. Carbohydrates tend to feel safer because they are very consistent in taste and texture. Protein sources, on the other hand, often vary more in texture and flavor.

One thing many people don't realize is that regular chocolate milk contains a significant amount of protein. If a client doesn't eat foods like chicken or beef, we might try adding a glass of chocolate milk to their meals to help increase protein intake.

As little known and understood as ARFID is, it often creates significant social challenges as well. Unfortunately, people tend to feel entitled to comment on what others are eating. When someone consistently eats the same foods or avoids certain foods, others notice and questions often follow: "What's wrong?" "Why do you eat like that?"

Imagine being an 11 year-old trying to explain ARFID to your peers. Even adults struggle to explain it.

In the documentary I mentioned, one woman shared that she only eats french fries. Another man who served in the Navy became so undernourished that medical staff initially believed the problem was psychological. Before ARFID was officially recognized as a diagnosis, many people found each other through online support groups. Somehow, they began connecting and realizing they were not alone.

In many cases, those communities were the first place where people with ARFID finally felt understood.

Key Takeaways

If we've spent years or even a lifetime being told how, when, and what to eat, it can feel nearly impossible to know what our body is actually asking for. But the way back isn't more control, it's curiosity, and learning to trust yourself again.

Healing from food rules isn't about replacing one set of rules with another, it's about slowly rebuilding trust in the body and moving away from external rules and toward internal wisdom. Food rules feel safe because they give the illusion of control, but most of them are built on fear of weight, fear of judgment, or fear of not being "good enough."

Restriction trains us to override our bodies' signals. Encourage your child to listen to their bodies by asking them what they are feeling in their bodies. Stability doesn't come from removing food. It comes from allowing it, consistently.

When restrictions are lifted, we may eat more of previously limited foods. That's not loss of control, it's the body catching up on permission. Stay steady through this phase. When access to these foods stays predictable and consistent over time, it will naturally stabilize.

Not all feeding challenges are the same. Unlike typical picky eating, ARFID (Avoidant/Restrictive Food Intake Disorder) can start at any age and is not "just a phase." It involves a serious restriction of foods that can lead to significant nutritional deficiencies, weight loss, or difficulty meeting expected growth patterns in younger children.

ARFID is still widely misunderstood, even by medical professionals who often receive very little training on eating disorders. Unlike many other eating disorders, ARFID is not driven by body image concerns, but typically related to sensory sensitivities, fear of negative experiences with food, or a lack of interest in eating. Healing isn't about forcing exposure or "just trying one bite," but building safety. When the body doesn't feel safe, it won't listen—and it won't learn.

TAKE ACTION

Throughout this book, you'll see sections labeled "Take Action." These are reflection-and-practice exercises designed to help you pause, think, and apply what you are learning to your own life.

You do not have to complete them perfectly. There are no right or wrong answers. The goal is simply to slow down, become curious, and reflect on your own experiences with food, body image, and parenting.

Some exercises may feel easy, while others might feel uncomfortable or bring up strong emotions. That is normal. Take your time, and move at a pace that feels manageable for you.

If you are doing these exercises with your child, focus on

creating a space of curiosity rather than pressure. The goal is not to force change, but to build understanding, autonomy, and trust over time.

You might find it helpful to keep a small notebook or journal as you move through this book so you can revisit your reflections and take note of how your thoughts evolve.

Take Action: Notice Your Food Distress

Grab a notebook or journal and start by making two lists:

1. Foods that feel the most distressing to you

2. Foods that feel the least distressing to you

Take a moment to think about what "distressing" means for you. What is it about certain foods that creates such a strong reaction?

For example, maybe you cannot stand soft cheese. Is it the smell? The texture? The taste? A negative experience you had with that food in the past?

Now think about foods that may have similar ingredients or nutritional qualities, but do not trigger the same reaction. What feels different about them? Why might they feel easier or safer for you to eat?

Finally, reflect on these questions:

- How can I explore different options around foods I feel unsure about?

- Am I open to experimenting with small changes?

- Are there foods I feel comfortable leaving alone for

now?

The goal is not to force yourself to like everything. The goal is to become curious about your relationship with food.

Take Action: Notice Your Food Experiences

Think about the foods you tend to avoid. Choose one food that feels mildly uncomfortable but not overwhelming and ask yourself: "What do I notice in my body when I think about eating this food? What thoughts come up? Is the discomfort related to texture, smell, taste, appearance, or a past experience?"

Write down what you notice. The goal here is not to judge your reaction. It is simply to observe it with curiosity.

Take Action: Create Your Food Hierarchy

In your notebook, create what is often called a food ladder, writing down foods from least distressing to most distressing.

Example:

Least Distressing:

- Peanut butter
- Crackers with peanut butter

Moderately Distressing:

- Peanut butter sandwich

Most Distressing:

- Peanut sauce on noodles

You do not have to start with the hardest foods. The goal is to begin with the least distressing option and gradually build comfort and confidence over time.

Take Action: Explore Without Pressure

Choose a food from the bottom of your ladder—the one that feels the least distressing–and instead of forcing yourself to eat it, explore it first:

- Look at the food
- Smell it
- Touch it
- Put a small amount on another food
- Try different brands or versions

Exposure does not have to mean swallowing the food right away. The goal is simply becoming more comfortable around the food.

Take Action: Support Your Body

If your food intake feels limited, it can help to think about ways to support your body nutritionally.
Ask yourself:

- What foods currently feel safe and reliable for me?

- Are there nutrients I might be missing?
- Are there simple additions—such as milk, smoothies, yogurt drinks, or supplements—that could help support my body?

The goal is not perfection. The goal is keeping your body nourished while you work toward expanding your comfort with food.

PART II:

THE MESSAGES THEY RECEIVE

Social Signaling Matters.

Chapter Five

Navigating Diet Culture

Diet culture is everywhere, and pretending it does not exist is not the solution. A more helpful approach is educating yourself about what actually works for you and your family in a sustainable way.

As a society, we have made progress in learning to accept differences among people. But there is still a great deal of work left to do. In many ways, we are still struggling to move beyond the instinct to judge what is different from us. When it comes to food and bodies, those judgments can be especially harmful.

Right now, we live in a culture that demonizes certain foods and moralizes eating habits. In doing so, we can unintentionally contribute to the development of disordered eating—not only in ourselves, but also in the children who are watching and learning from us.

For many of us, the first formal "education" we receive about food and movement happens in school, usually in PE or health class.

And if we are being honest, a lot of people carry a little bit of trauma from PE. For me, mile-run day still haunts me.

In health class, we were taught about "the food pyramid." Because that information came from school, we accepted it as fact. When you are a kid, you trust that what you are being taught is correct. So naturally, kids go home and repeat what they learned, and suddenly you have a child telling their parents, "Mom, Dad, we are eating bad food. We need to change everything. We are going to die."

The problem is not the nutrition education in and of itself, it's that the messaging is often overly simplified, moralized, or presented as rigid rules rather than guidance about balance and nourishment.

Messaging in school around food was often very fear-based. We were taught that if you eat poorly for long enough, you will develop diabetes, heart disease, and all kinds of health problems, and eventually, it will shorten your life. For kids, that can feel incredibly alarming.

Looking back, it also raises questions about who is actually teaching these lessons and where the information is coming from. In many schools, the person teaching health or nutrition is not a licensed dietitian or nutrition professional. Often it is simply a teacher or coach assigned to fill the class period. That was certainly the case in my school.

Today many schools teach the MyPlate model, which was introduced to replace the old food pyramid in 2011 (UAB Medicine, 2022). MyPlate attempts to simplify nutrition education, but it still leaves out many important pieces.

While an improvement, it doesn't reflect cultural diversity in food, presenting a very narrow picture of what meals are supposed to look like. In many ways, it feels designed around a very specific version of the "average" American diet.

But food culture varies tremendously across families and communities. For example, you're unlikely to see meals like refried beans, enchiladas, tortillas, or other culturally meaningful foods reflected in these models, even though they are staples in many households.

When children don't see the foods they eat at home represented in what they are taught, it can lead them to believe that their cultural foods are somehow "wrong." Many families have rich food traditions that are completely normal and meaningful within their culture, but are rarely reflected in formal nutrition education. Instead, these foods are often ignored, or worse, subtly shamed.

You see this play out in the real world all the time. Think about how often someone tries to make "healthy" versions of traditional foods, especially in cuisines like Mexican food, and in the process strips away what actually makes the dish culturally authentic (and more enjoyable!).

To be fair, the MyPlate model *is* somewhat more flexible than the old food pyramid. Instead of prescribing very specific foods, it shows general categories like grains, protein, fruits, vegetables, and dairy. In theory, this could allow room for cultural variation and open the door to conversations like, "What vegetables are common in your culture?" "What fruits do your families eat?" "What dairy products are typical in your household?"

What it really comes down to is how these models are presented. When only specific foods are labeled as "healthy," children may begin to assume that anything outside of that framework must be unhealthy or bad.

Over time, that messaging can turn into rigid, inflexible thinking. Kids start internalizing ideas about what "good" eaters do and what "bad" eaters do. Suddenly it becomes something performative, like proudly announcing "I eat rice cakes for my snack," because it's the socially approved choice.

Where Food Morality and Body Ranking Begin

With back-to-school season comes handouts and guidelines about what parents should pack for lunches and snacks. Many of these guidelines emphasize that snacks and lunches should be "healthy."

When I see that wording, it immediately makes me pause.

What exactly does "healthy" mean in this context? What is their definition? Is it based on sugar content? Whether the food is organic? The type of food itself?

The word "healthy" is incredibly broad, yet it is used constantly in everyday conversation. Over time, the word has taken on a heavy moral meaning. When parents read these school guidelines, many of them understandably think, "I want my child to be healthy, so I need to pack healthy foods every day."

But how many parents stop and think about what their child actually enjoys eating? How many ask themselves questions like, "What foods does my child like?" "What foods help them feel satisfied during the school day?" Or even, "What foods do I know they will actually eat?"

Maybe their child loves pizza. Maybe they love tacos. Maybe they want to eat mac and cheese every other day. So often, foods are filtered through a lens of judgment before we even consider whether they're a good option for that child.

Much of this confusion stems from decades of marketing and commercial messaging about food. Over time, these messages have shaped our beliefs about what "health" looks like in ways that are often overly simplistic and sometimes outright misleading.

Unfortunately, these ideas can contribute to disordered eating patterns for both parents and children. These labels can even become a source of bullying in schools. Children notice what other kids are eating, and have already learned to judge them. Foods labeled as "unhealthy" can quickly become something to shame or criticize.

When we become overly focused on labeling foods as healthy or unhealthy, we often stop asking more meaningful questions, like "Do I like this food?" "Does this sound satisfying right now?" "Will this help me feel full and energized?"

Shifting the focus away from rigid labels allows for a more balanced and realistic approach to eating. Instead of choosing foods based solely on whether they fit in the "healthy" category, we can begin listening to our bodies and teaching our children to do the same.

When children learn to connect their eating habits with how their bodies feel—whether they feel energized, satisfied, or full—they begin developing eating patterns that both sustain and support their overall well-being.

I once worked with a client whose family owned a dental practice. Interestingly, it is not uncommon to see eating disorders in professions that place a strong emphasis on health and appearance because there can be a lot of pressure around perfection and "fixing" oneself.

This client always made me laugh when he reflected on his childhood. He'd begin by saying something like, "Oh, my mom didn't really do anything unusual." Then a few minutes later he'd casually drop a story that made me pause and think, "Wait...what?"

One story he shared involved his elementary school. His mom became convinced that chocolate milk was unhealthy—not just for her own child, but for every child in the school. So she went to the school administration and pushed for chocolate milk to be removed entirely.

And somehow, it worked.

Chocolate milk disappeared for everyone.

No one revolted. No one protested. It was just...gone.

Around that same time, she also advocated for changes to the school's dessert offerings. What had previously been a daily option was reduced to Fridays only—and even then, it was usually something like fruit.

When he told me this story, I remember saying, "Yeah...that's definitely not typical. I'm sorry that something like that got taken away from you."

Incidents like that may seem small, but they can send powerful messages to children about food, restrictions, and what is considered Good or Bad.

Eating disorders are on the rise (Katella, 2021). And yet, we continue attaching labels and judgments to food—and teaching our children to do the same.

If we want to heal our relationship with food, we often have to begin by dismantling the belief systems we were taught. Many of those beliefs were not created with our well-being in mind. They were shaped by decades of marketing designed to influence consumer behavior.

Marketing exists to sell products. When food is labeled as "good," "clean," or "healthy," people are far more likely to purchase it. These labels create the illusion that choosing certain foods makes us better, smarter, or more responsible. In reality, attaching moral value to food often serves one purpose: Increasing profit.

Over time, these messages become deeply ingrained. The power those labels hold over us begins to feel normal. Part of healing our relationship with food involves recognizing where those messages came from and learning to loosen their grip.

And it starts with how we teach our children about food.

Young children typically do not attach value to differences at all. Whether those differences are racial, cultural, gender-based, or food-related, children see it simply as a neutral fact.

Those judgments and valuations are learned over time. And the way we talk about food, bodies, and health plays a powerful role in forming what becomes our children's beliefs.

By about five years old, children begin to notice differences more clearly, including differences between genders and bodies. They also start paying closer attention to the judgments they hear from the adults and peers around them. The messages they hear from parents, teachers, and friends begin to shape how they interpret the world. Because of this, who surrounds your child matters greatly. The beliefs and attitudes of the people in their environment can strongly influence how their own belief systems develop.

Around this age, many children begin to understand words like "fat" or "skinny." They also start attaching meaning and judgment to those words. Much like the labels we place on food, children begin to categorize bodies in similar ways: Some are good, and some are bad.

But they aren't born thinking this way.

They learn it because someone said it, and their developing minds absorb it—especially when those ideas are repeated and reinforced.

When children are placed into categories like "fat" or "skinny," the consequences can be significant. In elementary school settings, children whose bodies fall into the larger category are often more likely to be teased, excluded, or treated as different. Being positioned as an outsider during these formative years can affect a child's social development, confidence, and sense of belonging in meaningful ways.

There are many systems in society that influence how we think and behave. Social groups, peer pressure, and societal structures are only the tip of the iceberg. Other environments—such as sports, dance, and social media—can also reinforce powerful messages that shape how we see ourselves.

Social media plays a particularly large role in activities like dance and competitive sports. Three areas that often come to mind are ballet, dance, and gymnastics. In these spaces, there has long been an expectation that athletes must have a very specific body type to succeed—typically one that is slender and petite.

But that belief is not entirely accurate. People with many different body types can participate in and excel at these activities. Bodies may look different while performing them, but that does not mean they are any less capable. They may simply do it in different ways.

Around Christmas a few years ago, I attended a performance of The Nutcracker and happened to be seated in the front row (thank you, Friend!). I was pleasantly surprised to see so much body diversity onstage, and it was beautiful to watch. I had rarely seen anything like it before. Here was this large, professional production displaying a beautiful example of body diversity. It proved that anyone can participate in these art forms and that bodies can look different while still being strong, expressive, and capable.

Wrestling is another arena where body type is heavily emphasized. In this sport, athletes are expected to fall within very specific weight categories, and if they don't meet that number on the scale on tournament day, they cannot compete. Because of this, many varsity wrestling athletes focus intensely on their weight.

Some children who might otherwise enjoy wrestling never even try the sport because they don't feel their bodies fit the expected mold. Others who do participate may begin manipulating their weight in unhealthy ways in order to compete in a certain weight class. This kind of hyperfocus on a number on the scale can lead to maladaptive behaviors that may persist long after their participation comes to an end.

When young athletes learn to control their bodies solely to meet a certain size or number on the scale, it can contribute to long-term patterns of disordered eating that are much harder to address later in life.

I grew up watching figure skating and gymnastics with my mom. I was mesmerized by the control these athletes had over their bodies, but I couldn't help noticing something else: they all looked very similar. They were all thin, muscular, and petite. I remember thinking, "Wow, there must only be one body type for that—and it isn't mine."

It was quietly disheartening, even though I was too young at the time to fully understand why.

Growing up, I took dance classes and wanted to be good at it, but I just wasn't. Thinking about it now, I wonder how much of that had to do with my actual ability and how much was due to how dance classes made me feel. I remember always feeling like the biggest kid in the room and was almost always placed in the back of the formation.

I was told it was because I was tall, but looking back, it may have also been a way to make me less noticeable. The costumes were uncomfortable and rarely fit me well. They were designed for a very specific body type: a body type that was not like mine. I continued with dance because it made my mom happy, but I hated it.

It took me until adulthood to feel completely comfortable being the largest person at the table or in the room. Today, I feel confident enough in myself that it doesn't preoccupy me or prevent me from relaxing and enjoying myself, but for a long time it did.

Children can carry insecurities about their bodies for years because they feel different from the people around them. And many of those insecurities never needed to exist in the first place. There is so much more to a person than their shape and size. Learning to truly embody that belief has been a journey for me.

We want our kids to understand that we all have different bodies. Bodies look different, they have different needs, and all bodies are good bodies, no matter their shape or size.

When Bodies Change

Many people enter adulthood without any understanding of the growth curve their body naturally goes through. A huge gap in medical treatment from pediatrician to primary care means no one is monitoring our growth into adulthood, so we unfortunately think things like the "Freshman 15" –a phenomenon where kids gain weight in their first year of college–are about loss of control.

If growth was actually being monitored, we might find that that was a weight that they needed for their growth. At 18, we are still growing and developing. Yet for some reason it's been set in stone in our society that once you turn age of majority, you're never supposed to gain weight again.

As adults, the struggle to maintain your adolescent weight is framed as some sort of hero's journey, which is strange. You shouldn't be the size you were in high school when you are 50. That's not how things work. Our bodies change for many reasons throughout our lives. It's simply the body adapting. What matters most is whether your body can sustain the weight you are at without engaging in restrictive or compensatory behaviors.

It's been shown that people who can sustain their weight—even if that weight is higher—tend to be healthier than those whose weight constantly fluctuates (Massey et al., 2023; Zou et al., 2019). Rapid weight cycling, or yo-yo dieting, places significant stress on the body compared to staying at a stable, higher weight (Ochner et al., 2019; Rhee, 2017).

In the eating disorder treatment and recovery world, we have a term called a "well weight." Your well weight is the weight your body naturally settles at when you are eating consistently, moving your body in ways that feel good, and not engaging in maladaptive behaviors like binging, purging, restricting, or overexercising.

Even when my body was smaller, I wasn't necessarily happier. I was at my smallest after a severe gallbladder issue that made it extremely difficult for my body to digest food properly. I lost weight, but my new size wasn't sustainable in a healthy way. As soon as I returned to eating regular meals and snacks, my body moved naturally back to a higher baseline where it functions best.

My body changed even more when I was pregnant with my daughter, Olivia. The difference between that pregnancy and my first was that with Olivia I carried her for 39 weeks and five days, while with Harris I delivered at 33 weeks. Those last six weeks made a noticeable difference in both my body size and my mobility. We had newborn photos done, and when we got them back I remember thinking, "Wow, these photos are beautiful... and wow, I still look about 40 weeks pregnant.

I had literally just had a baby, but my first instinct was still to notice the size of my body.

Today, I am at a place in my life where I trust that my worth as a person doesn't change based on what I weigh. I am not any less lovable, likable, or capable because my body exists at one weight versus another.

But the way I judged myself after Olivia's birth highlights how unrealistic the expectation is that our bodies should remain the same throughout different seasons of life. Growing and birthing a human requires an enormous transformation and it was normal and logical for my body to change as a result.

For women, weight changes are often tied to hormones and stress. Our bodies naturally fluctuate throughout our lives with puberty, pregnancy, postpartum, perimenopause, and menopause.

During pregnancy, the body produces a hormone called relaxin, which allows it to stretch and adapt as the baby grows. After birth, relaxin returns to its pre-pregnancy levels, but (as the majority of us quickly discover) that doesn't mean your body simply returns to the way it was before.

Pregnancy can permanently shift the structure of the body. Your pelvis may widen. Your shape may change. Hips don't always return to their previous position. The same can be true for your ribs, breasts, and even your feet.

That last one tends to surprise people the most, especially those who love shoes. "Wait, my foot size won't go back?" No, probably not. But you did get a pretty great kid out of the deal, and maybe an excuse for a new shoe collection.

What's interesting is that when people notice their shoe size has changed, they tend to accept it and move forward. But when it comes to the rest of the body, we often resist. We push, restrict, and try to force our bodies back into a previous version, even when that version may no longer be physically possible. We refuse to accept it.

Bodies tend to follow their own natural pattern, and they usually stay around this curve throughout life. The challenge is that people don't always like the curve their body is in. They want to force themselves into a smaller curve, even if their body has always tracked higher.

Even the idea of body positivity can feel unhelpful. There will be days you might look in the mirror and simply not like what you see. That's okay and totally normal. Body positivity can feel invalidating to people who want to talk about or grieve the loss of your body, what it once was, and that it is okay to be sad.

Not every mother finds comfort in having this beautiful baby. It is okay to want the body you used to have. It's okay to want the old life you used to have. But if we don't grieve it and allow ourselves to go through that process, we will always hold anger and resentment toward whatever that thing was. Even your own children.

Imagine if it were normal to say, "Today is a tough body image day," without feeling pressure to immediately counter the feeling with forced positivity.

What if we could just say, "I feel uncomfortable in my body today, but I am still going to take care of it." Wouldn't it be healthier if that were the normal response?

The fact is, bodies change over time. That's just part of being human. Weight shifts, health shifts, life circumstances shift. None of those changes automatically erase someone's capacity for connection, intimacy, or partnership.

Of course, health can become more complicated at certain extremes. At some point, physical limitations can affect what a body is able to do. But that reality doesn't mean people in larger bodies cannot be healthy, fulfilled, or deeply loved.

Just because your body changes does not mean you cannot find love, sustain love, or build new love.

I wish that truth was talked about more openly.

The Stigma Around Weight

Our culture, the media, and often our own upbringing teach us that being fat means we are somehow less than, while being thin means we are more worthy. Those beliefs carry a great deal of shame.

People in larger bodies get treated differently everywhere: in school, at work, in medical settings, even within their own families. Even babies are judged for having baby fat, despite the fact that they *are* babies, and humans are *supposed* to have fat on their bodies. And all of this is based on the assumption that a larger body automatically means a less healthy one.

It's important to remember—and to teach our children—that every human body contains fat. Fat protects our organs, regulates temperature, and helps our bodies function. It is not something shameful; it is a biological necessity.

But a person's weight does not tell you what they are capable of. It does not mean they cannot run marathons, prepare balanced meals, experience joy, build fulfilling relationships, raise children, or excel in highly demanding careers. Weight is a poor proxy for health, character, or worth.

Unfortunately, media culture continues to reinforce these misconceptions. Television networks like TLC routinely sensationalize and glamorize fatphobia. This behavior is unethical and profitable. And because it is labeled "entertainment," it's seen as acceptable.

While there are instances when weight is a legitimate health concern, the over $160 billion diet and weight loss industry wasn't built on people looking to lose weight on a doctor's advice (Renew Bariatrics, 2024) Weight loss, in and of itself, is practically a sport in our society, with the weight loss "winners" being celebrated and the "losers" judged, critiqued, and shamed.

Living in a larger body is not a moral failure. But the shame, restriction, and body surveillance children experience when they're taught that their bodies must be controlled at all costs—that's what causes the deepest wounds. That's what follows them for life.

The "Almond Mom" Mindset

The term "almond mom" comes from an episode of the reality TV show Real Housewives of Beverly Hills, where Yolanda Hadid, mother of supermodels Bella and Gigi Hadid, tells one of her daughters to eat a "couple of almonds" and "chew them really well" to manage her hunger (Baskin et al., 2013).

In our meme-obsessed culture, Yolanda Hadid has come to personify this parenting approach to food, so perfectly illustrated in this iconic TV scene. But it's far from new. The "almond mom" mindset is a product of the constant moralizing and demonizing of food in our society.

Another way this mindset shows up is when people try to make a "healthy" or "skinny" version of recipes in ways that strip the food of what it's meant to be. For example, someone might substitute applesauce for vegetable oil. But applesauce isn't oil, and it can't do what oil is designed to do in a recipe. So the real question becomes, what purpose is that substitution actually serving?

This is something I talk about a lot with my clients. If applesauce is the only thing available in the house, then sure—work with what you have. But ingredients like fat are included in recipes for a reason. There is actual science behind why certain ingredients are used the way they are.

Fat contributes to flavor, texture, and satisfaction. If we had a food scientist in the room, they could explain exactly what role fat is playing in the chemistry of that dish.

The same idea applies to many "reduced-fat" foods. Reduced-fat crackers will never taste the same as full-fat crackers. And what often ends up happening is people eat more than they normally would of the reduced-fat version because their body is still searching for the satisfaction that fat provides.

When that satiation is missing, the body keeps signaling for more food. So instead of feeling satisfied after a portion, people may keep eating in an attempt to achieve that sensation. The more you restrict or limit a food, the more power it has, and the more likely you are to binge.

You see the same pattern with foods like low-fat yogurt, light salad dressing, or reduced-fat cream cheese and peanut butter. Sometimes the simplest solution is just to eat the full-fat version, feel satisfied, and move on. When food actually meets your body's needs, it often leads to feeling more fulfilled rather than constantly chasing something that never quite satisfies.

The low-fat movement really took off in the late 1970s and early 1980s. Suddenly everything was being marketed as low-fat:

low-fat yogurt, low-fat cookies, low-fat drinks, low-fat everything. Even today you see those labels all over the grocery store.

This phenomenon raises an important question: if the natural fat has been removed from a food, what has been added in its place? Often, it is additional sugar, refined carbohydrates, or other additives meant to compensate for the flavor and texture that fat normally provides.

What's always struck me as ironic about diet culture is how quickly foods in their original form are labeled as "bad," while highly processed diet products are accepted without much question. Someone might avoid a traditional food because it contains fat, yet willingly eat a packaged bar filled with ingredients they can't even pronounce.

Foods that are marketed as "healthy" are often some of the most heavily processed. And yet, because they fit within certain rules—low calorie, low fat, high protein—they're seen as the better choice.

Somewhere along the way, we stopped trusting food in its natural form and started trusting labels instead.

But this restrictive mindset wasn't born with Yolanda Hadid and not every "almond mom" is (consciously) motivated by weight loss or weight maintenance. Many parents are trying to make their households "healthy" by strictly controlling what foods are allowed. The focus becomes eating only the "good" fats, the "good" grains, the "good" proteins, which often end up meaning the lowest-calorie options.

Orthorexia Nervosa, often referred to as orthorexic, is not an official diagnosis but is widely used to describe when a focus on healthy eating becomes all-consuming. Individuals may struggle with food morality, assigning value to foods based on how "clean" or "pure" they perceive them to be.

The intention may be to create a healthier environment, but the message that comes across is that food is something to be tightly controlled and categorized as either "good" and "bad." Over time, that kind of thinking can shape how children relate to food and their bodies.

A closer look at many popular diet trends reveals a lot of gaps in the logic. The only time I would encourage choosing a "diet" version of something is if it's genuinely your preference—not because a rule or fear is telling you it's the "better" or more disciplined choice.

And even then, it's worth being mindful. Relying heavily on diet products can become a slippery slope, quietly reinforcing the same patterns we're trying to move away from.

If you give me a choice between Coke and Diet Coke, I'll choose Diet Coke just because I prefer the taste. Even if it had the same calories as a regular Coke, I would make the same choice. It is a preference on taste, not a rule of calories.

Recovery from an eating disorder often involves removing rigid food rules. It means allowing all foods to exist without labeling them as "good" or "bad," and learning to eat them in moderation, just as they are.

The goal is not to build a life around diet foods or restriction. The goal is to rebuild a relationship with food where all foods can exist without fear or moral judgment.

Key Takeaways

We live in a diet culture that judges bodies, demonizes certain foods, and moralizes eating habits. These judgments and messages can be deeply internalized and passed on without us questioning them and in doing so, we can unintentionally contribute to the development of disordered eating in ourselves and in the children who are watching and learning from us.

When eating stops being about nourishment or enjoyment and starts becoming a performance, kids learn quickly what earns approval and what invites judgment and begin choosing foods not based on hunger or satisfaction, but on what makes them look like a "good eater."

Yet much of what we believe about food isn't grounded in evidence. Rather, it is shaped by marketing, simplified education, and repeated messaging that disconnect us from what actually matters: How food feels in our body, whether it satisfies us, and whether it supports our needs.

Children aren't born judging body size, they learn it from us, from their peers, and the environments we place them in. Once those beliefs take hold, they shape how children see themselves, what they believe they're allowed to be, and whether they feel like they belong.

Bodies are not meant to stay the same. Fighting that change, and chasing a smaller version of ourselves at all costs, often creates more harm than the change itself ever could.

The more we try to control food, the more power it has. When we step back from the labels, the rules, and the judgment around eating, we are able to see food for what it actually is. By giving ourselves the permission to trust our body and our preferences, we give it to our children too.

Chapter Six

What They See and What They Hear

In the therapies I provide at Becca Allen Counseling, I often talk about social signaling. When we communicate, it is rarely the words themselves that carry the most meaning—it is the tone, the delivery, and the behavior that surrounds our words.

The concept of social signaling doesn't only apply to our peers or society at large. Showing is one of the most powerful forms of teaching–what we do often matters far more than what we say. This applies doubly when the communication is between parents and children.

Modeling Matters – A Lot

If you step back and ask the question, "What is a parent actually supposed to do?" many people would probably say something like, "Raise a decent member of society."

But we want more for our children than that, don't we? We want them to be happy, we want them to be good people, we want them to be emotionally stable, fulfilled adults.

But how do we do that?

That's a discussion for a whole other book (or ten), but there is one teaching method that all parents use, every single one of us, every single day, whether we realize it or not: Modeling.

Modeling is teaching by doing and it is often unconscious or unintentional. It is a good thing that we feel comfortable and "ourselves" with our children, that we're not thinking about everything we say and do and worry how we're being perceived. But as parents we need to remain aware that we are being perceived. Not with judgment, but in sponge-like observation.

This applies not only to our words and actions directed to our children, but the interactions we have with others, whether we realize they are observing at the time. Think about how often you listened in to adult conversations when you were a child. Why would you not assume your kids are doing the same?

My husband asked for a Ninja Creami ice cream maker for his birthday this year (we really like our ice cream around here), and almost immediately he started thinking about how to make lower-calorie ice cream. My response was simple: "If I want ice cream, I want real ice cream. I'm going to use heavy cream. If I want sorbet, I'll make sorbet—but not because it's lower calorie."

We weren't trying to set an example or teach our kids any particular lesson at that moment. But just by virtue of being in the same room together, that's just what we were doing.

Reflecting on it later, I realized that this casual conversation was meaningful on multiple levels. The ice cream itself was neutral—our discussion was about preferences, not food rules or labels. And our kids saw us listen to each other and express different opinions openly and safely. My husband didn't shame me for wanting full-fat ice cream, and I didn't judge him for seeing it differently.

Kids learn so much from these everyday moments. They're not just paying attention to what we say—they're learning from how we say it, how we respond to each other, and how safe it feels to share their own thoughts with us.

Remember, children make broad associations. They don't have the skills or maturity to recognize nuance. If they see you responding to other people judgmentally, they will extrapolate your reaction to their own potential conversations with you.

When parents talk about food with shame, worry, or strict rules, children take it as a lesson. They start to see meals as something to judge rather than enjoy. Over time, these quiet examples can shape a child's relationship with food much more than any single conversation.

Parents often talk casually about food, weight, or skipping meals as if it is no big deal—just a personal choice. But children often take those statements as truth. My younger clients will often share that it feels unfair they have to eat their meals and snacks when their mom or dad doesn't.

I have worked with families where an adult openly shared that they skip breakfast as a way to control their weight. To that adult, it was simply their routine. But to a child listening nearby, the message can sound very different. It can start to sound like eating breakfast is somehow wrong, which is often how food rules begin.

In one instance, the child then asked if they could skip breakfast too. The parent responded, "No, you need breakfast. I don't." You can imagine how confusing that must have felt, to see one set of rules modeled and another applied to them.

Many of us don't even realize what we are teaching our kids just by speaking our thoughts aloud. We don't recognize the impact of our comments because we don't see them as harmful.

But kids aren't just watching, they're listening too. To everything. They are quietly absorbing those messages and building their own rulebook around food. We want to be mindful that our actions and our words don't contribute to underlying anxiety, body image, or shame around eating.

I once worked with a family where I noticed a pattern that stuck with me: One of the younger children—around 11 years old—would repeatedly go up to her mother or grandmother, grab the skin under her arm, and ask, "Is this fat? Mom, is this fat? Grandma, is this fat?"

She asked the same question over and over again, and each time, the adults responded by saying, "No, that's not fat, that's muscle." While they were trying to comfort her, responses like this can actually reinforce the anxiety behind the girl's body checking. It sends the message that fat is something that needs to be denied or avoided, rather than something that simply exists on bodies.

Body checking is defined as the repeated overanalysis and surveillance of one's body through compulsive behaviors, such as examining specific body parts in the mirror, weighing yourself multiple times a day, trying on smaller clothes "to see if they fit," measuring and pinching your body, and constantly comparing your body to other people.

Body checking is an anxious response to deep-seated, negative feelings about the body, body image fears, or body dysmorphia, in an attempt to reassure oneself that everything is okay. Unfortunately, any reassurance is typically short-lived.

When those thoughts start looping, and the soothing behaviors repeat over and over, it erodes body image and self-esteem and can become a precursor to an eating disorder.

It's important to remember that we model, more than what we tell them, and teach our children what is normal, what is culturally appropriate, and what is acceptable. They watch how we react to change, how we talk about our bodies, how we approach food, how we handle mistakes, and how we treat other people. Every small interaction becomes part of the blueprint they use to understand the world. The comments we make about food can easily become the rules they carry with them for years to come.

None of us are perfect, as parents or human beings. We all get frustrated, distracted, and do or say things unthinkingly or automatically. Modeling isn't about getting everything right—it's about being aware that someone is always watching, learning what it means to be human from the way we show up every day.

What We Don't Do Is Important Too

In the old days, parents would say "Do as I say, not as I do." But this is simply not how kids' brains work. Kids learn by watching the people around them. They are absorbing and learning from not just our actions, but our reactions and our attitudes. Eventually, these will often become their own default behavior, reactions, and attitudes.

Modeling and teaching by showing isn't always done unconsciously. As parents we are also actively teaching our children how things are done. Sometimes they learn just by observing. Other times, they need to be shown how to do something. Parenting involves both.

For example, we have to teach kids basic skills like how to wash their hair and bodies in the shower. But even then, there is not only one "correct" way to take a shower. Maybe they wash their hair first. Maybe they wash their body first. Maybe that's the opposite of the way you do it. As long as they're getting clean, what does it matter? Why tell them they are doing it wrong?

Sometimes, it's what we *don't* do or say that matters.

It's important to show children that there can be more than one way to do things properly. When kids learn this early on, they are far less likely to feel anxious later in life when someone does something differently.

Not long ago I was visiting my dad and loaded the dishwasher—apparently committing a crime in the process. Within seconds, he was behind me rearranging every single dish like he was solving a high-stakes puzzle.

"You're doing it wrong," he said. "The dishes won't get clean that way."

I just stood there watching him completely redo it and finally said, "Dad... the dishwasher is brand new. I promise it can handle it.

He rearranged them anyway.

It's fine to have a preferred way of doing things, but that doesn't make it the only right way. Often, as in my dad's case with the dishwasher, it creates unnecessary effort and friction—and can even make it harder for others to help when there's a fear of doing it "wrong," especially when there are actually many ways to do it.

Sometimes families develop rules simply because that's how it's always been done. Over time, those rules can become rigid—even when they no longer serve a purpose.

Helping children understand that there isn't only one way or approach to doing things not only benefits them, it benefits us as parents too.

Allowing children to do things in their own way, as long as it's safe and the main goal or purpose is being achieved, builds confidence and increases their willingness to cooperate. And that just makes life better for everybody.

Modeling is as much about what you *don't* say, and how you *don't* react, as it is about what you do. By *not* correcting your child when they wash their feet first and their hair last, even though it makes no sense to you, you're teaching them tolerance and flexibility.

It's hard sometimes to bite back our automatic responses and consider the bigger and deeper message we're sending. Very little escapes our children's attention. They are constantly watching and processing the world around them.

Because of this, it is important to give them space to observe without shaming them for what they notice, or creating unnecessary negative judgments.

I remember one time when one of my kids was playing in my closet while I was getting dressed. They started poking my stomach and said, "Ooh, squishy!"

My immediate reaction was one many parents might have: "Don't say that, that's mean."

But the truth is, it was accurate. I mean, I've had two kids. My stomach *is* squishy.

Adults filter their thoughts before speaking–children do not yet have that same restraint. My child wasn't being mean, just making an observation. If I respond with shame or embarrassment, or label their comment as "mean," I'm saying that being squishy is a bad thing. I am teaching them that bodies like mine are something to hide or feel bad about. When in fact, it's completely normal.

If my kids never see my cellulite or my stretch marks, if I constantly hide those parts of myself because I'm embarrassed, or don't want them to fear becoming "fat," I am actually doing them a disservice. How will they learn what normal bodies look like if I am always hiding mine?

Modeling works best when it happens without shame.

How we respond–and how we *don't* respond–in moments like this is how children learn what is normal. Over time, those small moments shape the way they understand their bodies, their choices, and their place in the world.

Gentle Parenting and Your Role in Your Child's Life

I am not a "gentle parent." Honestly, I would probably end up on the five o'clock news if I tried to adopt that approach perfectly. But there are some concepts from gentle parenting that I think are really helpful—especially when it comes to reducing the amount of shame and guilt that gets placed on children.

The weight of that guilt that families will put on children is astounding. And the impact of that doesn't just disappear. Many people carry those messages with them well into adulthood.

Think about how many adults struggle to say no because they were taught growing up, "You always show up for your family. That's just what you do."

As children, they were shamed for choosing themselves or not always accommodating what others wanted from them. As a result, they grow up apologizing constantly—even when they have done nothing wrong–and internally carry a constant sense of guilt.

That's not to say shame never has a place: in certain therapeutic contexts, it can help people recognize when something truly harmful has occurred. But in everyday life, shame is used far too often.

Parents have vastly different beliefs about discipline. Like food rules, the way we discipline our children is often based on how we were disciplined by our own parents: the "It worked on me!" approach. But *did* it work for you? Did you really learn to do or not to do whatever they were shaming you about? Or did you just learn to hide your actions (or failure to act) so that you weren't shamed for them?

Another example of a "traditional" approach to discipline that in fact does more harm than good is physical punishment. In many families, spanking or other forms of physical punishment is justified as a way to correct behavior.

Like shaming, we now understand that physical punishment doesn't create meaningful or lasting change in behavior. Instead, it often teaches children to fear their caregivers—physically or emotionally—and can push them toward becoming extreme people-pleasers or more secretive in their behavior.

Fear and compliance are not the same thing as learning.

Effective discipline doesn't require shaming or physical punishment, but it does require clear boundaries and roles. A child is not meant to be their parent's best friend, and parents are not meant to be their child's best friend either.

A parent's role is different. Your child should not be the person you lean on to vent about your spouse or complain about adult problems. When parents begin to blur those roles—trying to be both a parent and a friend—it can create confusion for the child.

And when that dynamic shifts and the parent needs to enforce a rule, the child may feel confused: "Wait, I thought you were my friend." Worse, they may not respect the parent's attempt to impose discipline because they view themselves as peers.

That creates difficulty for both the parent and the child. Clear roles help children feel safe, supported, and guided, without placing them in a position they are not developmentally ready for, or really meant to hold.

Key Takeaways

What we model becomes our children's normal. Modeling isn't about perfection, it's about awareness and the recognition that every interaction with our children–how we eat, how we talk, how we respond–becomes part of their blueprint.

Our children learn not only from the words and actions we direct towards them, but from the interactions we have with others. They're learning from how we say what we say, how we respond to each other, and how safe it feels to share their own thoughts with us.

Children don't have the skills or maturity to recognize nuance. When they hear us talking about food with shame, worry, or strict rules, children start to see meals as something to judge rather than enjoy. Over time, this shapes their relationship with food much more than any single conversation.

Modeling is as much about what you *don't* say, and how you *don't* react, as it is about what you do. By *not* correcting your child when they approach or perform tasks differently than you do, you're teaching them tolerance and flexibility.

Allowing children to do things in their own way, as long as it's safe and the main goal or purpose is being achieved, builds confidence and increases their willingness to cooperate. Helping children understand that there isn't only one way or approach to doing things not only benefits them, it benefits us as parents too.

Chapter Seven

Lead with Curiosity: Opening Up Conversations With Your Child

Conversations open up the opportunity for connection with our children. Leading those conversations with curiosity helps them feel safer and more comfortable sharing in general and grow a healthier sense of self.

As parents, we are the first teachers our children have when it comes to understanding bodies. And if those conversations don't happen at home, they will happen somewhere else—through peers, social media, or the internet. And what children learn there is not always accurate, helpful, or aligned with the values we want guiding them.

Kids are naturally curious. They're going to learn about bodies and relationships one way or another. And if we act like these topics are too uncomfortable to talk about, we unintentionally send the message that they shouldn't come to us with their questions.

It's very similar to how some parents approach conversations about sex. Many people remember the awkward "birds and the bees" talk—or remember never having it at all. A lot of parents avoid the conversation because it feels uncomfortable.

But if we don't teach our kids about bodies, relationships, and the changes they experience, someone else will.

Using Conversation to Reframe Ideas

When your child comes home repeating something they've learned about food, how are you responding?

My son came home one day and suddenly started labeling foods. Carbs were bad. Cookies were bad. Chips were bad. Everything he liked best seemed to fall into this "bad" category.

I was surprised. Where was all this coming from? My first instinct was to figure out who was teaching my kid that kind of messaging. When I asked him, he couldn't tell me, or maybe just didn't want to say.

Instead of getting stuck on that, I tried shifting the conversation into something more neutral and informative. When he said cookies were bad, I explained that cookies are mostly carbohydrates, and our bodies actually need carbohydrates for energy. He also said soda was bad, even though he likes soda. So I told him, "It's just soda. It's a drink. It is something we might have sometimes and not all the time, but it is still just a drink."

The goal wasn't to argue with him or shame him for repeating what he heard. It was to reframe the conversation so that food was not divided into Good and Bad, but understood in a more balanced and neutral way.

By making my language neutral, I shifted the conversation away from labeling foods, which at the end of the day are often just opinions. Neutral language creates space for a more balanced understanding of food.

Calling a food "bad" can make your child feel like they should avoid it completely. But most foods aren't bad in the sense that they are harmful or spoiled—they are simply foods. They are neutral.

Retraining and redefining messages that someone else may have taught your child about food can be difficult. A grandparent or another adult in their lives may say something about a particular food or food group not being healthy, or tell them, "You shouldn't eat that."

When your child comes home repeating those ideas, responding with something like, "Grandma doesn't know what she's talking about" or criticizing how someone else eats is usually not helpful (as tempting as it may be).

Instead, try responding with something like, "Different houses have different rules," and explain that people and families eat in different ways. In your home, you might value balance, cultural foods, variety, or enjoying meals together. What works for your family is what matters in your household. This helps children understand that other families and people in their lives may do things differently, and that it is not their job to become the food police.

Even if you need to pause at some point and revisit the conversation later, it's important to address these moments when they come up. Kids are simply trying to figure out who they are and how the world works. It makes sense that they repeat what they hear. But when the messaging around food continues to be framed in rigid or moral terms, it makes things more complicated for them.

Instead of reacting dismissively or with frustration, approach the conversation with curiosity. Taking a moment to calmly ask questions like, "Tell me more about that. What class did you learn that in today?" or "I wonder why they labeled it that way?" opens the door to a more thoughtful conversation.

Curiosity invites learning, while judgment tends to shut it down. So when we respond with curiosity rather than criticism, we help interrupt the cycle of misinformation instead of unintentionally reinforcing it.

It is also important that we don't only show excitement and curiosity for the foods we've labeled as healthy, like fruits and vegetables. I want my kids to feel the same level of interest and support whether they are trying a new fruit or happily licking the icing off a spoon while baking.

The goal is not to demonize one type of food while praising another. Food is just food. Unfortunately, many of us have been conditioned by our culture to do just that. We give enormous praise when a child eats fruits or vegetables, but may respond with criticism or concern if they have dessert a few times in one week.

Over time, those reactions send a message that certain foods make them "good" and others make them "bad." But the reality is that these choices can all be part of a balanced relationship with food.

Listening to and Respecting Your Child's Story

Eating disorder behaviors are often coping mechanisms. For many, they begin as something that feels like the one area of life they can control.

No one starts down that path thinking, "I hope this takes over my life to the point where I cannot function without it." Instead, the thought process is often something like, "I don't have control over what's happening around me, but I can control my body. I can control what I put in my mouth. I can control what goes into my system."

Most parents aren't trying to give their child an eating disorder; they're trying to protect their child from pain. Unfortunately that often takes the form of dismissing their child's feelings or moving reflexively into fix-it mode, rather than helping their child learn how to tolerate uncomfortable feelings in the body they have right now.

When you signal to your child that they are less than for whatever reason, time and time again, they will eventually distance themselves from you in order to protect their peace and mental health. This hurts the parent as much as the child.

I once worked with a client whose case ultimately required me to testify in court. They came into my office at 16 with a long-standing eating disorder that had begun in early adolescence. They had already been through higher levels of care and were discharged to outpatient treatment with me.

As I learned more about their history, I discovered that their mother—a physician—had put them on Wegovy, a high-dose injectable weight-loss medication typically prescribed to adults with specific cardiovascular risk profiles. I was stunned. Putting a teenager with an eating disorder on an appetite-suppressing medication felt far more dangerous than any restrictive dieting or food rules I had seen in other families.

When I questioned the mother about it, she said calmly, "They were just samples. I wanted to see if it would help."

"Help what?" I asked.

"Help her lose some weight," she said. "To build confidence."

That assumption—that a smaller body automatically produces confidence—is one of the most damaging myths we pass down. Using a pharmaceutical intervention to suppress a child's appetite in the name of confidence crosses a line that should never be crossed. I also couldn't help but wonder whether professional boundaries had been breached. What does it say about a medical provider when their license is used to make their child smaller?

I know lines can blur for parents who work in medicine. A parent might bring home allergy samples for a child with severe allergies without a second thought. But this was different. And what shocked me most was how normal it seemed to her.

This mother was consistently harsh about her child's weight and played a significant role in the development and maintenance of the eating disorder. She reinforced—repeatedly—that worth was conditional, tied to body size and compliance. Ironically, she did not embody the physical ideal she demanded of her child, which only deepened the contradiction.

The family system was one of the most toxic I have ever worked with. The parents were divorced and locked in a prolonged custody battle. By the time I became involved, they had already been to court multiple times.

I stated clearly that I believed the child had more structure and a better foundation for mental health by living primarily with their father. On the stand, the mother's attorney aggressively challenged me, suggesting I was attempting to "take a daughter away from her mother." The goal was clear: Discredit me, intimidate me, and undermine my professional judgment.

At that point, the client was only six months away from turning 18. The judge ultimately allowed them to choose where they lived. Wanting to avoid upsetting their mother, they chose to keep the existing arrangement for the remainder of high school. After graduation, they moved out of state for college. Their father relocated to the same city and provided housing over the summer before they moved into the dorms.

The reason my client preferred their father was not because

he had been perfect–he had not been. Early on, he encouraged excessive exercise and enforced rigid food rules. But he repaired his relationship with his child. He listened. He acknowledged harm and apologized. He worked to rebuild trust.

He also provided a structure—chores, expectations, consistency— that had been absent in the mother's home.

With the mother, there was freedom, but not safety. Their relationship was largely transactional, maintained through money rather than emotional connection. Eventually, my client realized, "I do not want anything from you. You make me uncomfortable. You always tell me I am not enough."

During this period, my client changed their name and began identifying as non-binary. In court, the mother refused to use their chosen name or pronouns. She dismissed it entirely. "You will grow out of this," she said. "This is just for attention."

But the reason someone chooses different pronouns, changes their name, or explores their identity is not the point. What matters is whether we listen—or whether we override a child's internal experience, again and again.

My client's mother was hurt that her child did not want to be close to her. I wanted to say to her, "You don't give them any reason to want to be close to you. You tell them they are fat, that they are not worthy. You tell them their name is not proper. You are constantly saying all of these things. What red light needs to come on for you to understand why your kid does not like being treated this way and does not want to spend time with you?"

The father struggled at first, but he made the effort. He understood that if he wanted a relationship with his child, he needed to listen.

This story is not really about weight-loss medications, custody battles, or pronouns in isolation. It is about what happens when adults repeatedly refuse to listen to a child's internal cues—physical, emotional, and relational.

In this particular family, the eating disorder was not the original problem. It was an adaptation. It was my client's nervous system's attempt to regain a sense of control, safety, and coherence in an environment where their internal experience was denied.

My client's father changed the trajectory not because he was flawless, but because he listened. He allowed his child's experience to matter, even when it was uncomfortable or unfamiliar. That is what rebuilding trust looks like.

Approaching Uncomfortable Conversations

It breaks my heart when I hear stories of someone coming out to their parents as LGBTQ+ and being met with rejection or even being cut off completely. If either one of my kids came to me with something that vulnerable, I would feel honored that they trusted me enough to share it.

As both a parent and a therapist, it's incredibly painful to sit with clients who have gone through major identity shifts—whether in their early teens or in college—and were met with anything but support. Instead of being seen, they were dismissed, minimized, or rejected. And when that happens, the impact doesn't just stay in that moment—it shows up elsewhere.

Allowing people to express their emotions is how they learn about themselves. It's how they move through fear, disappointment, and self-doubt.

Too often, we try to tell our kids they do not feel what they are feeling, or that their feelings are unnecessary or inappropriate. You see this happen all the time; as a parent, I have been guilty of it myself. A child will fall and scrape their knee. Then the parent will rush up to them and tell them, "You're fine, you're fine, you are fine."

But what if they're not fine? What if they're scared? What if they're in pain, but you're overriding their emotions by telling them they are fine? When we don't give children space to express discomfort, we're sending a powerful message. Over time, they learn, "I shouldn't express these emotions. I'm supposed to be fine."

When a parent or caregiver listens to a child, rather than immediately jumping into problem-solving mode, it can make a world of difference.

I think back to my grandmother, who was a profound influence in my life. One summer after graduating college, I made a decision I now recognize as wildly ambitious. Feeling invincible, I enrolled in several prerequisite courses for graduate school– Biology II, Chemistry I, and Physics II–during a single summer term.

Unsurprisingly, I received my first "F" that summer. You can connect the dots on why I made a sudden career switch from the sciences to counseling. Clearly, my talking skills exceeded my skills in formulas and numbers.

Looking back, it's almost funny, but at the time, it was devastating. When I got the grade back, I went straight to my grandmother's house in tears. "I am such a failure," I told her. "I'm never going to get into PT school. I'm never going to do anything."

And do you know what my grandmother did? She didn't lecture me. She didn't ask why I would do something so foolish. She didn't offer solutions or point out what I should have done differently.

She sat with me. Quietly. She let me cry. She let me feel what I was feeling. And when she finally spoke, she simply said, "We are going to get through this."

The contrast with the conversation I had later with my mother was striking. My mom immediately asked, "Okay, how do we fix this?"

Her intentions were good, but her instinct was to solve the problem. And while problem-solving has its place, it isn't always what someone needs in the middle of emotional pain.

When emotions are running high, advice can feel like dismissal. What we often need most is to be heard—without judgment, without urgency, without someone rushing us toward a solution.

This is exactly why many people come to value good therapists. Therapy is often the only place where someone can fully express their emotions without being told, "You should have done–or should do–A, B, and C." Therapy offers a space for vulnerability without performance, without correction, and without pressure.

I often tell parents that if they want their children to trust them with hard conversations, they have to show they can handle them—without shaming, dismissing, or rushing to fix things.

It's not always easy. As the parent of a child who is very emotionally expressive, it's hard at times not to react by telling him, "You are overreacting."

The better a child (or any person) can express their emotions, the more likely their needs will be met and the better others will understand them. Sometimes the best thing a parent can do is simply listen. There is so much growth that happens when a child feels heard.

So often, when a child shares uncomfortable feelings, the instinct is to jump into problem-solving mode. A parent might respond with something like, "Well, let's start eating differently so no one says that again." The intention is to take the pain away—but the message the child receives is that their body is the problem that needs to be fixed.

Now imagine a different response. The parent pauses and says, "That sounds really hard. Tell me what happened." Instead of trying to change the child, they stay with the child. And that shift matters.

When a child is trying to share something vulnerable, it's important not to minimize their experience by saying it's "not a big deal," "just a phase," or shifting the focus to your own story. Especially when the message becomes, "I got over it, so why can't you?"

That response, even if well-intended, can be harmful. It can leave a child wondering if something is wrong with them—if they're just not strong enough to get better. By comparing their own experiences with food or body image to their child's struggles, parents may unintentionally make it harder for that child to feel understood—and to heal.

Eventually, the child will learn not to bother sharing uncomfortable feelings, or perhaps any feelings, with the parent at all. Once kids start holding back, it becomes a habit and the older they get, the harder it is to break.

Over time, the child may even internalize the message that their uncomfortable emotions and experiences are something to be disregarded. Ignoring discomfort is not helpful. What they're feeling and expressing is a real emotional response, and it deserves space to be acknowledged.

How powerful would it be for a child to feel safe enough to say, "I don't like my body. It feels different from my friends' bodies. I wish I could change it?" And instead of jumping in to fix it, the parent simply listens—really listens.

So how can we talk openly about discomfort—how it shows up and how we learn to navigate it—without trying to change the child in response to that discomfort?

Well, it's simple–but not easy. Whether they're sharing a shift in gender identity, or their feelings about being called "fat," you can talk about it. You can talk about the hurt, the unfairness, and the way society places so much pressure and judgment on bodies. You can allow them to experience their discomfort in full.

Life is full of uncomfortable situations and it's important for children to learn how to manage those feelings and recognize that they'll come out the other end in one piece.

If your child asks, without prompting or external pressure, for help making changes in themselves, that's a completely different conversation and should never be in the context of losing weight, "belonging," or becoming more acceptable to others. We can hold space for our child's emotions while still protecting them from harmful solutions.

You don't have to be a perfect communicator to be a good parent. You just have to be willing to stay in the conversation—being present, honest, and open. What matters most is that your child knows they can come to you with the hard things, instead of feeling like they have to figure everything out on their own.

Conversations Create Connection

Conversations support our children physically and emotionally. They strengthen the pathways in the brain, which supports their physical development, and create connection by making them feel safe, seen, and valued.

When we engage in open, non-judgmental conversations, we're building emotional security and fostering trust through active listening, validation, and curiosity. This encourages our children to share their feelings and thoughts more freely.

My son Harris is the kind of kid who notices when someone says they are cold or their stomach hurts and immediately goes to get a blanket or offer a hug. That sensitivity is part of what makes him who he is.

Our society's standards regarding how boys in particular express emotions discourage emotional fluency–especially around sadness, fear, or insecurity. Boys are told to "man up" or that "boys don't cry." But I don't want my son to become hardened because his emotions are seen as weakness or less manly. I want him to learn that all emotions are legitimate and how to express them effectively.

A few years ago, my husband Scott's grandmother passed away. Since then, the family has been slowly cleaning out her condo—the tiniest place imaginable, yet somehow filled with a lifetime of things. When my husband drives the kids to school in the morning, they pass by Meme's old place.

One morning, completely out of the blue, Harris told Scott, "I love driving by Meme's house in the morning. It reminds me of her."

My daughter Olivia would probably never say something like that. She has one of the most vibrant personalities I have ever seen, a complete spitfire—full of joy, emotion, and intensity. Harris, on the other hand, is my sensitive and thoughtful little soul. He speaks straight from his heart.

Those qualities are part of who they are, and I believe those traits will serve them in different ways throughout their lives.

If we try to reshape those parts of them to fit some idea of who they should be, we risk getting in the way of their developing identity. If I were to tell Harris that he is "too sensitive," what he would hear is that sensitivity is something he should suppress.

Children learn who they are through the messages we give them. It would genuinely hurt me for the rest of my life if I ever felt like I had played a role in changing who he is because I was trying to follow some societal rule that boys should not be sharing their feelings.

Becoming a parent has opened my eyes to things I never thought about before. It has made me realize just how much influence we have in shaping how our children see themselves.

At the core of my parenting values is protecting my children's sense of self and giving them the space to grow into who they truly are.

Key Takeaways

Conversations open up the opportunity for connection with our children. Leading those conversations with curiosity helps them feel safer and more comfortable sharing in general and grow a healthier sense of self.

When your child comes home repeating messages that someone else may have taught your child about food, it's important not to respond with judgment. Instead, shift the conversation into something neutral and informative, and help them understand that other families and people in their lives may do things differently.

When we engage in open, non-judgmental conversations, we're building emotional security and fostering trust through active listening, validation, and curiosity. This encourages our children to share their feelings and thoughts more freely.

As parents, we are the first teachers our children have when it comes to understanding bodies. Kids are naturally curious and if those conversations don't happen at home, they will turn to their peers, social media, or the internet for answers. However, what they learn from those sources will not always be accurate, helpful, or aligned with the values we want guiding them.

When we behave like these topics are too uncomfortable to talk about, we unintentionally send the message that they shouldn't come to us with their questions. How you respond teaches them what's safe to say out loud.

If we want our children to trust us with hard conversations about bodies or anything else, we have to show we can handle them without shaming, dismissing, or rushing to fix things. Listening—really listening—is what builds trust.

You don't have to be a perfect communicator to be a good parent. You just have to be willing to stay in the conversation—being present, honest, and open. What matters most is that your child knows they can come to you with anything, trusting they won't be alone in it or met with fear of getting in trouble.

PART III:

BREAKING THE CYCLE

Moving From Fear and Control to Curiosity, Compassion, and Change

Chapter Eight

Moving Away From Judgment

Addressing Weight Bias

To break the cycle of judgment around bodies, we first have to acknowledge the stigma that exists around weight.

When you look at the research on weight stigma, you start to see just how deep our society's obsession with body size runs. Weight judgment is arguably the most widespread form of judgment placed on another person, and it connects directly to fatphobia. Research and lived experience repeatedly show that two people can apply for the same job with identical qualifications, or even with the person in the larger body having more to bring to the table, and the person in the smaller body is still more likely to be chosen (Giel et al., 2010).

From a medical perspective, weight is often treated as the primary problem. Many patients are told—explicitly or implicitly—that their body size is the cause of most of their health issues, even when that is not actually the case. This reflects a broader cultural bias toward larger bodies. Weight stigma, at its core, is the judgment placed on people because of their body size.

There are many advocates who speak powerfully about weight stigma and the harm it causes. One story that has stayed with me came from an advocate who shared that when she was a young adolescent, her doctor handed her a diet plan. That moment—being told that her body needed to be fixed—was the beginning of a long struggle with disordered eating. What was presented as medical advice eventually snowballed into something much more harmful.

If we truly want to break the generational cycle of eating disorders, we have to address weight stigma directly. We have to stop signaling that someone's body is wrong simply because it is larger.

Weight stigma is not just about hurt feelings. It has real consequences. Research shows that stigma affects people's health behaviors, treatment outcomes, and mental health. Clinicians who work with adolescents have emphasized that recovery must address weight stigma and consider each person's natural growth pattern rather than forcing everyone to meet rigid BMI (Body Mass Index) targets (Peebles et al., 2024).

Studies on how we talk about body size also demonstrate that our language shapes how people see themselves and can influence their health and behavior (Robbins et al., 2025). Stigma is not limited to direct comments. It shows up in medical guidelines, everyday language, and the implicit beliefs our culture holds about which bodies are acceptable and which are not.

I see how these messages affect people all the time. I was in a private reformer Pilates class recently, which has been a new experience for me since September. I had never used a reformer machine before, so I've been learning as I go.

At one point, the instructor was trying to explain that some movements might feel more challenging for me because I am tall. The mechanics of the machine interact differently with longer limbs. But she seemed incredibly uncomfortable explaining it. She kept circling around the explanation, almost apologetically, as if she was afraid she might offend me.

The interesting thing is that I was not offended at all—I was just confused about what she meant. Her hesitation actually made the explanation harder to understand.

Even if something were more difficult for me because of my body size, that would be okay. Bodies have different mechanics. But the discomfort around talking about bodies can sometimes make communication more complicated than it needs to be. And on a deeper level, the very fact that talking about bodies is uncomfortable sends a message that bodies are something to be uncomfortable about.

My assumption at first was that the exercise felt difficult because I had not worked out in a long time and my core strength was still recovering from two abdominal surgeries. In reality though, the challenge had more to do with my height and the way my body interacted with the machine.

Being tall was something I hated growing up. In school it made me stand out in ways I did not always like. But as an adult, it has often been an advantage. That experience reminded me how complicated our relationship with bodies can be—and how much our culture struggles to talk about them without attaching judgment.

Leading With Compassion

Often, people place a high value on being kind to others but struggle to extend that same kindness to themselves. In reality, we need compassion from ourselves just as much as we need it from the people around us.

Part of that compassion is allowing ourselves the space to be imperfect—and accepting that as normal. Instead of constantly striving to be better, to do more, or to fix what feels different, we can begin to recognize that our quirks and imperfections are part of what makes us who we are.

Those differences are not flaws. They are simply pieces of our identity. When we approach those parts of ourselves with kindness instead of criticism, we create room to accept ourselves as we are rather than constantly trying to reshape ourselves to meet someone else's expectations.

The truth is that people are either going to like us or they are not. What matters most is showing up authentically from the beginning and trusting that who we are is enough. If someone doesn't connect with us, it doesn't mean we've done something wrong. Sometimes it simply reflects another reality we cannot control: You and they just didn't click. Learning to accept that can be incredibly freeing.

True change through body acceptance doesn't have to look like the body positivity movement. The only option is not simply loving your body all the time. There are many different ways to build a healthier relationship with your body.

For some people, body neutrality feels more realistic. For others, it may simply be learning to treat their body with respect, even on days when they do not particularly like it. There isn't just one path.

Being compassionate to ourselves and accepting our bodies can be incredibly difficult because it means going directly against the messages we have been taught our entire lives. It can feel like swimming upstream, constantly pushing against the current. It is hard work, and the truth is, it doesn't get much easier. Even when you make progress, you are still moving against norms that have been deeply embedded in our culture.

Over time, though, you develop skills that make the process easier to navigate. This is especially true in eating disorder recovery. Even when someone is in recovery, it does not mean the distorted thoughts disappear entirely. That can be a difficult truth for people to accept. Many wonder, "Why am I doing all this work if the thoughts are still there?"

The reality is that recovery is not about eliminating every intrusive thought. It is about learning how to respond differently to those thoughts.

As the brain becomes nourished and clearer, people become more skilled at recognizing those thoughts for what they are. They learn not to engage with them or allow them to take control. But when someone is malnourished or engaging in harmful behaviors toward their body, they often assume that once those behaviors stop, all the mental side effects will disappear as well. Some do improve. But not all of them vanish completely.

What does change in recovery is your ability to manage them. The further along you get, the more confident you become in using the tools you have learned. You start recognizing the thoughts earlier. You interrupt them sooner. You understand that a passing thought does not have to turn into an action.

Recovery does not mean you will never have a hard day or a moment where you look in the mirror and think, "I don't like my body today." Certain experiences or environments may still trigger those feelings.

The difference is awareness. You begin to notice when your body image, self-esteem, or internal judgments start shifting. And with that awareness, you gain the ability to respond with intention rather than letting those thoughts take over.

Control and the Pursuit of Thinness

When things feel out of control, people often look for other ways to regain a sense of control. This is often how eating disorders begin. When life feels chaotic or overwhelming, controlling food intake can become a way to cope with what feels uncontrollable.

So then, the dominant message in our culture becomes all about control and the pursuit of thinness. But where did that idea come from in the first place?

For hundreds of years, up until the twentieth century, larger bodies were associated with wealth and power. Having a fuller body signaled that someone had access to plentiful food, resources, and leisure time. You can often see this reflected in paintings and photographs of wealthy individuals from earlier time periods.

Over time, cultural preferences shifted. When the “flapper" look emerged in the 1920s, rejecting Victorian-era curves, thinness became the new standard of beauty. Today, models and celebrities are often praised for having what is described as the “perfect” body—one that is extremely small, lean, and tightly controlled.

Children and teenagers (and we adults!) are constantly exposed to images and messages promoting this beauty standard. They watch the praise that these bodies receive and begin to absorb the idea that this is what beauty is supposed to look like.

The problem is that only a small percentage of the population is naturally predisposed to that body type. Most people simply do not have the genetics to achieve, much less maintain an extremely thin frame. Even models themselves adhere to extremely restrictive diets and strict exercise programs in order to maintain their “perfect” bodies. Yet the message we receive is that if these bodies exist, anyone should be able to achieve them.

We can manipulate bodies into many shapes. People can restrict food, push their bodies through intense exercise, take diet pills, or use medications like GLP-1s designed to reduce weight. But just because something can be done does not mean it should be done, or that it is healthy or sustainable over time.

Most people's bodies can't sustain a "model-thin" appearance while also remaining healthy. Yet we're conditioned to believe this is something we should strive for and that being thinner will make us more accepted, more loved, and even happier with ourselves.

What makes this belief especially powerful is how family, friends, and community often reinforces it—sometimes without even realizing it. When someone moves from a larger body to a smaller one, they often report being treated differently: receiving more compliments, more positive attention, and even more respect. Many people describe hearing praise they had never heard when they lived in a larger body.

The way society responds to smaller bodies versus larger bodies can be incredibly damaging. While it is possible to unpack these experiences in therapy and help individuals process them, the issue is much bigger than any one person. It reflects a deeply ingrained cultural mindset about body size and worth.

Many patterns of disordered eating begin with the belief that life will be better if someone becomes thinner. People often assume that weight loss will solve their discomfort with their bodies–but that is rarely how it works. Just because the outside world celebrates a smaller body doesn't mean that the person living in that body is healthier or happier.

You cannot heal body image simply by changing the size of your body. The underlying message—that happiness will come once you lose weight—remains the same mindset that created the struggle in the first place.

One thing I consistently hear from my clients who lose weight is that it did not heal their negative body image. They may be living in a smaller body, but the disordered thoughts and patterns around food and their body are still there because the root of the issue was never addressed.

This is true for many dysfunctional behaviors. Changing a behavior and changing the mindset behind that behavior are often two very different processes, but both are necessary if someone wants to create lasting change.

The reality is that you cannot control everything in life. Even with the best plans in place, unexpected things will happen. You can't control traffic. You can't control other people forgetting things or making mistakes.

In the same way, controlling food intake will never fix the pain someone is experiencing elsewhere in their life. It only redirects it. The struggle that led someone down that path in the first place is still there.

Without addressing the underlying beliefs and thought patterns, the struggle simply follows the person into whatever body they happen to be living in next.

To help with this struggle of acceptance, there are many powerful books that share people's lived experiences with eating disorders. One that comes to mind is *When Food Is Love,* written by Geneen Roth in 1991. It is an older book now, but the story still resonates today.

In it, the author describes her journey through disordered eating and her struggle with binge eating. She becomes convinced that if she can just become thin enough, she will finally find love and acceptance. So, she engages in increasingly disordered behaviors, all in pursuit of the belief that being thinner will solve her problems.

What she ultimately discovers is that the underlying pain never disappears. She is still miserable, still depressed, still anxious—just living in a smaller body (Roth, 1991). Her story is a powerful reminder that changing the size of your body does not automatically heal the deeper emotional struggles that led there in the first place.

By the end, the shift is not about finding the "right" way to eat, but about turning toward those deeper emotional experiences with awareness and compassion. Rather than continuing to chase control through food or body size, she begins to recognize that her relationship with food has been a way of coping with unmet needs and disconnection. The work becomes less about fixing the body and more about understanding and caring for herself in a different way.

It can be incredibly difficult to challenge these beliefs. When someone is malnourished, their brain is not functioning at full capacity. Malnutrition affects cognition, making it harder to think clearly and critically evaluate the thoughts running through your mind. In that state, it can feel completely believable to think, "Everything will be better if I am skinny." But the reality is that your body size and the way you feel about yourself are not always connected.

It's exhausting being around people who are fixated on body size. Even when they're complimenting you, it still feels unnecessary and a little invasive, as if your body is being analyzed. Because it is.

When comments are made about your body, it is hard not to internalize them. Especially if it's coming from a parent or romantic partner.

In some relationships, one partner may withhold love in subtle, controlling ways that pressure the other person to maintain a certain appearance. I've heard variations on this type of manipulation many times in my work, like a husband telling his wife, "I'll buy you a whole new wardrobe if you get back to your pre-baby size."

These types of unsettling comments are sadly more common than you may think.

Love that is conditional on maintaining a particular lifestyle or body type is not love, it is control. Teaching someone that they are only worthy of love if they look a certain way is deeply harmful, sending the message that their value as a person is tied to the size or shape of their body. In many ways, it is one of the cruelest messages someone can internalize.

Messages about controlling bodies and maintaining a certain appearance are everywhere: in conversations at home, in media, in social circles, and in everyday interactions. Some version of a strained relationship with body image, food, or movement exists in many households.

At the core is the fact that many people struggle to feel secure in who they are. Whether it's their personality, their body, their appearance, or their identity, a lot of people grow up without a strong sense of self-acceptance.

We like to say that our society values diversity, but we do not always make space for it in practice. Being different—especially in terms of body size—can still be treated as something negative.

Someone living in a larger body may move through public spaces with an added layer of awareness that others don't always have to think about. It's not about insecurity as much as it is about navigating a world that often isn't designed with their body in mind.

They might think about:

- Is movement safe or scrutinized? (Walking into a room or gym, ordering food, or eating in public.)
- Will I fit here? (Chairs with arms, booths, airplane seats, waiting room seating.)
- Will this space feel comfortable or exposing? (Tight walkways, crowded rooms, clothing options.)
- How will I be perceived? (Anticipating judgment, stares, or assumptions about health, habits, or character.)
- Will my needs be accommodated? (Medical equipment, blood pressure cuffs, gowns, or even towel sizes.)
- What comments might be made? (From strangers, providers, or even well-meaning people.)

Over time, this can create a constant mental load, where neutral situations require more planning, emotional energy, and self-awareness. It's not about being overly sensitive, it's about adapting to repeated experiences in environments that haven't always been inclusive or respectful.

Many people in socially acceptable bodies move through public spaces without ever thinking about their size. It is not something they have to consider when walking into a room, sitting in a chair, or interacting with others. But for someone in a larger body, that awareness can be present almost all the time.

In many ways, it becomes a constant calculation—similar to how someone living with a chronic condition must remain aware of their body throughout the day. That level of awareness is not something everyone has to carry, but for many people in larger bodies, it becomes an unavoidable part of navigating the world.

I worked with a freshman in college who shared that at 17, her parents had supported her in having plastic surgery to change her body in a way she hoped would help her feel more comfortable with herself. Initially, she told me she had undergone a breast reduction, which I can understand, as larger breasts can cause significant back pain and physical discomfort. But she also shared that she had Lipo 360, which at the time I had not even heard of.

I asked her how having these procedures at such a young age had impacted her body image, her relationship with food, and the way she felt around other people. What she told me might surprise some, but to me it was entirely predictable: Nothing really changed.

She was still deeply unhappy in her body and was able to acknowledge that openly. While the breast reduction improved her physical comfort, which absolutely mattered, it did not change her relationship with her body or how she saw herself.

Now, I am not inherently against procedures that improve someone's quality of life. But going through a major surgical procedure at 17, with parental consent and medical approval, while already struggling with body image distortions, only to come out of it feeling exactly the same emotionally, says a lot. The conditions of her body had changed, but her feelings about it had not. The root of the problem had never been addressed.

Something interesting to consider is how your relationship with your body might change if you began to view the differences in your body as something unique rather than something to fix. What if the things that make you different are also the things that make you special?

Think about birthmarks or moles. My daughter has a birthmark on her lower back. It makes her body uniquely hers. Everyone has these kinds of markers—little constellations of moles, freckles, or birthmarks that belong only to them. They are completely normal and beautiful reminders of individuality.

When we think about our bodies and our relationship with ourselves, it can be helpful to consider where we draw the line between improving our quality of life and chasing something that may not actually exist. That line can show up in many ways: Trying to maintain a weight that your body cannot comfortably sustain, following a diet that is not realistic long-term, or committing to a workout routine that takes more from you than it gives back.

Where that line exists is a personal decision. For me, it often comes down to quality of life. Is what I am doing contributing to my well-being, or is it draining me in pursuit of something unrealistic?

For example, for about seven years I have struggled with chronic migraines. After trying multiple medications and meeting with different specialists, I eventually found something that worked well and had little to no negative side effects: Botox.

It helps manage a physical symptom that causes me significant discomfort, but the injections also happen to smooth my forehead, which I can appreciate. In that sense, it serves both a medical and aesthetic purpose.

Botox is less invasive than cosmetic surgery, but it still qualifies as a procedure that can enhance appearance. If my migraines miraculously disappeared one day, yes, I probably would continue getting Botox for cosmetic reasons. But it would simply be about maintaining a smoother forehead, not trying to chase a younger version of myself or meet an unrealistic standard.

This is why conversations around cosmetic surgeries and procedures cannot simply become a tit-for-tat comparison of what is acceptable and what is not.

Ultimately, it has to come down to what genuinely improves someone's quality of life and helps them feel more at ease in their own skin—authentically, not out of pressure to meet someone else's standard.

Getting to a place where you can accept that your body, *is* your body is where the foundation of a stable relationship with your body begins. Finding a place of neutrality, and learning to care for your body from that place, is incredibly important.

When we approach our bodies with neutrality or gratitude, we begin to care more for them because we want them to function well. That mindset is very different from only meeting basic needs while feeling frustrated that your body is not the size or shape you wish it were.

This is where credentialing in the wellness industry matters. Many people in the wellness space present themselves as experts without formal training or credentials. They offer directives about how you should look, how you should live, and what will supposedly make you happy. But the truth is, they cannot know what that looks like for you. That understanding only comes from taking the time to explore your own relationship with your body and discovering what genuinely supports your well-being.

TAKE ACTION

Grab your notebook again and take a moment to reflect.

Think about one thing you do for your appearance. Why do you do it? What is the motivation behind it?

If it's that you get your nails done, what is driving that choice? Do you genuinely enjoy it? Does it make you feel good? Or are you doing it because you feel like you should, or because of how others might perceive you? Would you feel comfortable without it? Would your confidence change?

What about your skin? Tanning, for example. I went through a period where I was incredibly tan—almost orange. Looking back now, I am horrified that I would intentionally burn my skin just to achieve that look because I believed it made me more attractive.

Now ask yourself: How can I begin to build acceptance around the things I feel compelled to change?

The goal here is to build a framework that moves away from judgment. When we release some of our need to control and instead approach ourselves with curiosity and kindness, we create the conditions for real growth. That growth can happen within ourselves and ripple outward into how we treat others.

When we respond to the urge to control with curiosity rather than rigidity, we create space for change.

Trying to control our bodies and appearance often gives us a false sense of control. In reality, the harder we try to control everything, the more we are confronted with the fact that many things are simply outside of our control.

You could follow the exact same diet and workout routine as someone whose body you admire. You could do everything perfectly. But you will never have that exact body because you do not share their genetics, their biology, or their life circumstances. There are limits to what we can control.

So the question becomes: what might you gain if you allowed yourself to accept that you cannot control everything?

Grief Work

As a therapist, I find myself working with grief every single day. My speciality is not traditional grief, related to the loss of a loved one, but grief that is tied to the quiet, often overlooked losses that occur within everyday life.

People experience many kinds of grief that are rarely acknowledged as grief at all. Postpartum transitions, the loss of their "old life" before children, dissonance between the expectations and realities of parenthood, processing a difficult or unexpected birth experience, and the loss of their former body in size, appearance, or capability are all treated as things people are simply meant to "get over."

I end up doing grief work with nearly all of my clients because it is such an important part of healing. In order to move forward, we often have to acknowledge and process what has changed. This often involves processing the loss of an idea or an experience we once held.

For many people, grieving the loss of a body they once had becomes a significant part of that process. The body you had at 18 is not the body you have at 25, and it will continue to change as you move through different stages of life.

It is okay to feel sadness about that. It is okay to miss a body that once felt familiar or easier to live in.

For me, it was letting go of the image I once had of what motherhood would look like. Among all the emotions surrounding Harris's birth, one of the strongest was anger that the birth experience I had imagined—the one I had pictured in my mind—was completely taken from me. None of what I thought would happen actually happened.

I never imagined that my baby would come early. I never imagined that I wouldn't get to hold him until he was three days old. I certainly never imagined giving birth during a global pandemic.

So many of my expectations about becoming a mother for the first time simply were not met. The moments I had pictured—the ones I had looked forward to—were replaced by something entirely different.

For a while, I tried to push those feelings aside. I told myself I should just be grateful that Harris was okay. I thought maybe feeling angry meant I was being ungrateful or dramatic.

But that's the tricky thing about grief. When we try to ignore it or minimize it, it doesn't actually go away. It just sits there, waiting until we are finally ready to acknowledge it.

Looking back, I can see how much anger I was carrying during that time. I held on to that anger for a long time—longer than I probably needed to. In truth, it took me more than six months to even admit to myself that I was angry.

Once I allowed myself to admit that I was angry about the birth I didn't get, and the experience I'd always imagined being taken away, it became easier to start processing those feelings instead of fighting them.

The anger I was feeling was really grief, mourning an experience I had long held in my heart.

The longer we have held on to an idea or experience, the more difficult it can be to process its loss. This is especially apparent when the loss involves de-idealization of a parent.

When we're young, we idealize our parents. They are our first experience of love, care, and protection. They are authorities on everything. They shape how we understand the world.

But at some point in life, most people begin to realize that their parents are not perfect. Sometimes they even cause harm, which can be incredibly difficult to process.

This is often the case for my clients whose parents encouraged dieting or strict food rules that directly contributed to their body image struggles or eating disorders.

These parents didn't intend to hurt their children. They'll say things like, "I thought I was helping them," "I didn't think bringing them to Weight Watchers/pushing them to run five miles was going to hurt them," or "I thought it would help them build confidence."

For my clients, part of moving forward from their grief is accepting that the people they trusted most were doing the best they could, with the information they had—even though it hurt them.

When we do not allow ourselves to grieve, if we push the feelings down or try to ignore them, they rarely disappear. They usually come back later, often when we least expect it.

When my parents separated when I was 11, my reaction was surprisingly neutral. I remember thinking, "Okay. This is happening. It's fine." At the time, it genuinely did not feel like a big deal.

But years later, when I went to college at Texas Tech—Wreck 'em—something shifted. Being there was an incredible experience, but it also brought up feelings I had not expected.

Texas Tech is a very family-oriented place. Families show up for everything—football games, parents' weekend, celebrations. And being surrounded by that environment made me realize something I had not allowed myself to feel before: The absence of the family structure I thought I would have. I did not have two parents coming together for parents' weekend the way many of my peers did.

That realization made me deeply sad. All of a sudden, the grief I had not felt at 11 showed up when I was 21. The feelings had simply waited until I was ready to process them.

That's the thing about suppressed emotions: They don't disappear. They return eventually, often when something triggers them.

Grief cannot be forced, and it cannot be rushed. But it has to be allowed.

Stages of Grief

The stages of grief are often described as a journey. But it's a journey that looks different for everyone.

In the grief and loss world, there is no single structure that fits every person. Many models exist, and they all offer helpful insights, but people move through grief in their own way. What works for one person may not work for someone else.

You may be familiar with the commonly referenced stages of grief—things like denial, anger, bargaining, depression, and acceptance. These frameworks can be incredibly helpful for some people because they offer language and structure around emotions that can feel overwhelming.

For some people, walking through those stages can feel incredibly validating. It helps them understand what they are feeling and reminds them that their reactions are normal. For others, the framework simply does not resonate. They may not move through the stages in that order, or skip some stages entirely. Others may revisit the same stage multiple times. Still others don't relate to that model at all. That does not mean their grief is any less real.

Grief is deeply personal. It is vulnerable and often very private. Because of that, it is important to be thoughtful about who we share it with.

Sometimes when we open up about grief, people unintentionally invalidate the experience. They may downplay it, or try to relate by sharing their own story and in doing so, they shift the focus away from the person who's grieving.

What most people actually need is what I like to think of as a grief buddy. Someone who can sit with you in the discomfort, without trying to fix it or redirect it.

A grief buddy simply listens and validates. They might say something like, "That sounds really hard. I'm sorry you had to go through that."

They do not immediately jump in with comparisons like, "Well, my mom's third cousin once went through something similar," or "I know exactly how you feel."

Sometimes the most powerful form of support is simply sitting with someone in the mess of their emotions and letting them feel what they need to feel.

I hear this from my clients all the time. When they try to explain to friends what it is like to live with an eating disorder, the response they often get is, "Oh yeah, I get that." But the truth is, most people really don't get it.

An eating disorder is incredibly difficult to articulate to someone who has never experienced it. From the outside, people often think they understand because they have struggled with food or body image at some point. But the reality of living with an eating disorder is much more complex and consuming than most people realize.

When someone responds with "I get it," it can unintentionally feel dismissive. Not because the person means harm, but because the experience is so much deeper than what most people imagine.

Honestly, I think one of the reasons I'm able to be a supportive validator for my clients is because I have learned so much from them. Over the years, clients have trusted me with their experiences, their thoughts, and the way their eating disorder shows up in their daily lives.

Through those conversations, I've developed a much clearer understanding of what that internal experience can feel like. It doesn't mean I know exactly what it is like for each person, but it allows me to respond in ways that resonate with them.

And many times when I reflect something back, clients will say, "Yeah, that actually feels pretty close to what it's like."

Being able to sit with someone in that space—without assuming, minimizing, or trying to fix it—is often one of the most meaningful parts of the work.

Comparisons and Acceptance of Grief

After Harris's birth, people would often say things like, "You should connect with another NICU mom."

I understood the intention and reasoning behind these suggestions. But at the time, the idea of sharing NICU stories with another parent felt unbearable. In fact, if I knew someone else had a child who had been in the NICU, I would sometimes go out of my way not to mention that Harris had been there too. I didn't want to compare experiences or revisit those stories.

I didn't feel connected through that experience. I didn't feel understood. And I certainly didn't feel heard. Instead, I often felt like people were trying to relate in ways that completely missed what I was actually feeling. It left me with this constant sense of frustration, like no one really understood me.

You can't compare loss stories. Loss is not apples-to-apples. What people need when they are grieving is not comparison or advice—they need a supportive ear.

People compare experiences for many different reasons. Sometimes it comes from insecurity, sometimes from an attempt to motivate themselves, and sometimes it is simply the brain trying to find a reference point. When there is no clear standard, the brain naturally looks for a measuring stick.

Social comparison theory, first described by Leon Festinger in 1954, explains that people often judge themselves by comparing their experiences to others when clear benchmarks are missing. More recent research suggests that this tendency can influence emotional well-being.

In five studies involving 1,669 participants, individuals who were more sensitive to negative social comparisons reported higher levels of stress, anxiety, and depression, and that sensitivity predicted increased depressive symptoms over time (Mishra et al., 2026).

Comparison happens everywhere, constantly. We compare bodies, intelligence, careers, relationships—almost everything. Yet most of the time, comparison leaves us feeling like we're losing something rather than gaining anything meaningful.

Hearing another person's story can remind us that we are not the only ones who have gone through something difficult. It can soften the feeling of being completely alone in our experience. The key is to make space for their story while still recognizing that your experiences are not the same.

When we recognize this, and avoid comparing our experiences, feelings, and ourselves with others, we open the door to acceptance. Acceptance of loss brings us closer to our pain, but it also moves us closer to living again.

There are elements of loss woven in nearly every part of our lives, because the expectations we create in our minds rarely unfold exactly the way we imagine them. But sometimes, while the thing we expected doesn't happen, something else does.

Loss has led many people—often through very painful circumstances—to discover a deeper sense of purpose. You hear powerful stories of individuals who have endured unimaginable hardship and somehow found a way to create meaning or light from it.

Through the lens of eating disorder recovery, it is common to see something similar. Many people who move through that experience develop a deeper sense of curiosity and compassion, both for themselves and for others, because they have lived through the loss of control and discovered new ways of relating to themselves. It often becomes a turning point, shaping how they choose to move forward in the world.

Key Takeaways

Judgment around bodies runs deeper than most of us realize. It shows up in casual conversations, in doctor's offices, and in the way we look at ourselves and others.

The way society responds to smaller bodies versus larger bodies reflects a deeply ingrained cultural mindset about body size and worth and can be incredibly damaging. Children and teenagers (and we adults) are constantly exposed to images and messages promoting this beauty standard.

Research shows that weight stigma has real consequences, affecting people's health behaviors, treatment outcomes, and mental health. If we want to break the generational cycle of eating disorders, we have to address weight stigma directly. We have to stop signaling that someone's body is wrong simply because it is larger.

Many patterns of disordered eating begin with the belief that weight loss will solve our discomfort with our bodies–but that is rarely how it works. You cannot heal body image simply by changing the size of your body. If the underlying mindset that created the struggle remains.

We often place a high value on being kind to others but struggle to extend that same kindness to ourselves. We must allow ourselves the space to be imperfect, and accept that as normal instead of constantly striving to be better, to do more, or to fix what feels different.

Healing isn't about eliminating every hard thought or forced positivity. It's about learning to treat our body with respect. When we stop trying to change our body and start accepting it, a more stable relationship can begin.

Finding a place of neutrality, and learning to care for our body from that place, is incredibly important. In order to heal and move forward, we often have to acknowledge and allow ourselves to grieve the loss of the body we once had or hoped to have.

That grief is real, even if no one ever named it that way. If we don't allow ourselves to process our loss, it will return eventually. Grief cannot be forced, and it cannot be rushed. But it has to be allowed.

Chapter Nine

My Story: What Protected Me, What Put Me at Risk

I often find myself wondering what protected me from developing an eating disorder. When I look back, there were many factors in my environment—and even genetically—that could have pushed me in that direction.

In adulthood, I know one of my biggest protective factors has been my husband. But when I was a child, he obviously wasn't there yet. So I've spent time thinking about what may have helped protect me earlier in life.

One thing I keep coming back to is my mom. She had what you could consider an average American woman's body, and she didn't hide it. Even if she had her own thoughts about wanting to make her body smaller through food, she still existed openly in her space.

Now, verbally, there were definitely moments where negative body talk existed. But in her actions, there wasn't the same sense of shame. She didn't hide her body, and that mattered.

When I compare that to my sister, the contrast feels almost jarring. Even now, as adults, I can't step into a dressing room with her—her body language shifts, and she instinctively moves to cover herself, as if being seen is something to avoid.

And I find myself wondering, "What are you covering up?" We both have bodies. We share many of the same features most people do. And yet, the relationship we each have with our bodies couldn't feel more different. Even within the same family, the way we learn to see ourselves—and allow ourselves to be seen—can take entirely different shapes.

I often wonder why certain things protected me but did not protect my sister. Why did she develop a different relationship with her body than I did, even though we had the same mother modeling for us?

We have different brains, of course, but we grew up in the same home and shared the same environment. In my memory, though, my dad was actually harsher on me than he was on her when it came to our appearances.

From as young as five, my mom had me in dance. That meant I was constantly surrounded by other girls' bodies, and I was very aware that mine was different. My sister, who is two years older than me, was smaller than I was, and even as a child, I noticed that difference.

I remember at our private school we had student IDs that included our weight, which is wild to think about now. Even though my sister was two years older than me, I remember weighing four pounds more than she did, which stuck with me.

I was always in a bigger body, though sometimes that difference was softened by the fact that I was also tall. Still, I remember there being a lot of fear around labeling my body as "fat."

Generational patterns around food and body image exist in the eating disorder world too. Sometimes they show up in subtle ways—being told you are "just a big girl" or "just tall." Those phrases can carry a lot of meaning depending on how they are delivered.

I don't remember anyone explicitly teaching me how to feel about my body, how to eat, or what balance with food looked like. What I do remember is noticing the way my dad talked about bodies.

No matter what size my body was, I never felt my mom's love for me change. But my dad would make comments about my body often, and those comments stuck with me.

In our household, there was a confusing dynamic around food. Food would be pushed toward us, but then there were also comments that implied that if you ate too much, it meant something was wrong with you.

Looking back, it is clear that my dad never had a healthy relationship with food himself. For him, that pattern was normal.

I remember being taught that food was either Good or Bad. There was no middle ground. Food existed in these two very clear categories.

But, no one ever explicitly restricted food from me, nor did anyone ever tell me to eat a salad or go on a diet. But we also did not grow up in a house that had snacks around. If we had snacks, it was usually at my grandma's house. And when I did get them, it felt like a dopamine rush.

As I spoke about earlier in the book, when certain foods are only available in very small amounts or very rarely, they become more exciting. When you finally have access to them, it is easy to go all in because you do not know when you will get them again.

I asked my mom many times growing up why we did not have snack foods in the house. Looking back, my best guess is that it had more to do with her relationship with food than with anything about us. Even now, she still struggles with having snack foods in the house.

I do not think it was about trying to control us. I think it was more about her trying to control herself.

She would say it was because snacks were expensive. But honestly, I never fully believed that explanation. We had our own computer by the time we were 12, which makes it hard for me to believe that snacks were ever truly out of reach financially.

What I do remember is that I was never particularly obsessed with food growing up. I was not constantly asking questions about what I could or could not eat. The problem, in my mind, was never the food, it was my body.

Of course, the reality is that food and body size are connected—food is how our bodies gain or lose weight. But the commentary around me was always focused on the body itself.

In elementary and middle school, I was the bigger kid. By high school—at least as I remember it—I was in the largest body I had been. That was also the first time I had access to all the foods I wanted, and with that access came a sense of freedom I hadn't experienced before. But when I got to college, that relationship with my body began to shift.

By the time I reached college, access to food had normalized. The novelty had worn off—it was no longer something exciting, just something that was consistently there.

College felt different from the years before. I still had access to all kinds of food, but for the first time, I also had access to a gym. I had a roommate I loved working out with, and we walked everywhere. Movement became part of our routine—something social, something shared, something that felt natural.

My freshman-year roommate—who is still one of my best friends to this day—had grown up playing sports and being active all the time. She was from a small town outside of Lubbock, Texas, where kids often participate in multiple sports growing up. For her, working out was just a normal part of life.

Being around her introduced me to a completely different relationship with movement. Exercise wasn't punishment. It wasn't about fixing your body. It was simply part of a routine.

We never worked out with the intention of losing weight. It was just something we enjoyed doing together. But that was the first time in my life that I lost weight, and I noticed that I liked it—not because I was chasing thinness, but because I suddenly felt more comfortable in my body. My weight stabilized naturally, and something shifted socially as well.

The dining halls also changed my relationship with food in subtle ways. There were balanced meals available every day, and you knew the food would always be there. It was not like before, where certain foods felt scarce or special. When you know food will be available again tomorrow, there is less pressure to overdo it in the moment.

For the first time, I had a relationship with movement, food, and my body that was not hyper-focused or overly complicated. Things just existed in a kind of balance.

Then suddenly, when I graduated from college and moved back home, my gallbladder stopped working. My mom, who is a nurse, initially thought the pain I was experiencing was just gas. In reality, I had an entire organ dying.

I still joke with her about it to this day—that I had a whole organ failing and she told me it was probably gas. I hope you're reading this, Mom.

Eventually, I had to have my gallbladder removed. The surgery itself was one thing, but the recovery and aftermath were much harder than I expected.

I was told that once the surgery was done, my digestion would return to normal, but that didn't happen. Instead, I would eat and almost immediately get sick afterward. I tried to follow the digestion diet they gave me, but my body simply couldn't tolerate much of anything.

As a result, I lost a significant amount of weight and was borderline malnourished.

But, even though I was sick and struggling physically, people constantly praised how good I looked. All I could think about, though, was how terrible I felt. It was a lot to take in.

At one point, my dad told me he was proud of me for building a healthier relationship with food, but that wasn't what had happened at all. I hadn't suddenly developed better eating habits, I simply couldn't tolerate many foods anymore.

For a while, I couldn't eat gluten or dairy. My diet became incredibly limited—often just boiled chicken and rice. And with that came a lot of sadness.

Food had always been important to me. In many ways, food felt like life. It brought joy, connection, comfort, and filled spaces that other things sometimes couldn't. So, losing that relationship with food was incredibly painful.

It took almost ten years for my body to truly stabilize after everything I went through. For a long time, I maintained that lower weight—but not because my body was thriving. It was simply because my body had been through so much.

After some time, I went on to graduate school, which is when Scott came into the picture. He became my new workout buddy. Our workout dates became a way to spend time together, exploring different types of movement and enjoying the rhythm of it all.

Eventually, we moved in together and settled into a stable rhythm of adult life—having the time to make meals, go out, work, study for grad school, and follow a consistent workout routine.

Even though my body was never what society would call "small," I remember feeling good in it during that time.

I had reached a place of acceptance. I understood that my body was never going to fit into those smaller sizes, and I had made peace with that.

I'm not exactly sure what led to that sense of acceptance. Maybe it was rebuilding my relationship with food after everything my body had been through. Or maybe it was young love.

On our wedding day, I remember feeling truly good in my own skin. For the first time, I felt like I had fully stepped into myself as an individual. I had an identity, and I was building a life of my own.

It wasn't about achieving some kind of "dream body." It was about feeling secure in the body I had. There was a sense of calm acceptance—this deep feeling of okay-ness with myself.

I had finally made peace with my body. This was the body I was given, and it was enough. I felt secure in a way I had never experienced before—grounded, settled, and content. I lived in that space for a few years, until I became pregnant with my first child.

After having children, I realized something I had never experienced before: Weakness in my body. Not the way people casually talk about weakness, but a very real, physical kind of weakness.

I've never considered myself a sports person, but I also wouldn't describe myself as sedentary. I'm someone who is always moving—going places, picking things up, organizing things around the house. But after having kids, my body felt different. And more than anything, I just wanted to feel strong again.

My core had become so weak after my C-sections that my back began compensating for it, and eventually the pain became constant. It was frustrating because it reminded me of pregnancy, when I was constantly told what I could and couldn't do with my body. I wasn't pregnant anymore, but I still couldn't do the things I felt my body should be able to do.

One day I walked a mile and was completely winded, when there was a time when walking five miles was nothing for me. The way I thought about my body shifted. Earlier in life, when I focused on my body, it was usually about weight. Now it wasn't about weight at all. I just wanted to feel strong again. My weight is going to be my weight; what I care about now is whether I can carry my kids, haul in groceries, or move things around the house without pain.

After two C-sections, my body had been through more than I think I fully understood at the time. Surgery changes your body in ways that aren't always obvious right away. At 32 years old I remember thinking, "I have so much life left ahead of me. Why does my body already feel like this?"

For a while, I caught myself comparing my body to what it used to look like, and that comparison never helped. But, what did help was something simple: Clothes.

During pregnancy and postpartum, my body was constantly shifting, so I gave myself permission to buy clothes that made me feel good. I probably spent more money on clothes during that time than I ever had before, but it genuinely helped.

What I realized during that time was the difference between clothes that fit, and clothes that *feel* right.

My first Mother's Day after having Harris, I was able to wear jeans again. I put on a button-down shirt and did a little front tuck, and suddenly I felt like myself again. Not because my body had gone back to what it used to be, but because I could recognize myself in the mirror. I had my style back, which was a meaningful part of my identity and helped me feel like me again.

Motherhood changes your body, but it also changes your life. Overnight, you go from being completely independent to having almost none of your time belong to you anymore.

It's something I think we should talk about more honestly. Motherhood is hard. It's exhausting. And sometimes it feels unfair that our partners often still have more control over their time than we do.

Even with support, parenting is hard. I think there's a misconception that if you have enough help it won't feel overwhelming. But in my experience, everyone struggles in their own way.

After my pregnancies, the hormonal shift also affected my mental health more than I expected. I had done therapy before, but I had never needed medication. I was able to manage with skills and support.

After pregnancy and birth though, that changed. My hormones threw me into a loop I had never experienced before. I was constantly angry. Rage was the emotion that showed up the most, and that wasn't who I wanted to be.

When Harris was about six months old, I finally admitted I couldn't manage it alone. I needed therapy again. I needed medication. I needed support. Postpartum depression showed up for me as sadness sometimes, but also as intense anger. When I had Olivia, those feelings resurfaced again, as did the anxiety.

In those early months I remember thinking, "This shouldn't feel this hard. What is wrong with me? Why can't I handle this better?"

My anxiety with Olivia postpartum was different, but even higher because she was born deaf in one ear. I couldn't handle it when we first found out. It was an entirely new world that I knew nothing about, and I felt completely overwhelmed.

At that point I realized something important: I wasn't going to let my mental health destroy my relationships with my kids, my husband, or my life.

I used every resource available to me. Thankfully, I had a doctor who was open to working collaboratively and helped me find solutions that actually worked for my body and mind.

What I've come to understand is that protection isn't one single moment or message, it's a series of small experiences, interpretations, and internalizations that accumulate over time. Two children can grow up in the same home, hear the same comments, and still walk away with entirely different beliefs about themselves. Not because one was more loved or more seen, but because each of us is constantly filtering the world through our own nervous system, temperament, and meaning-making.

Maybe what felt like pressure to one of us registered as motivation to the other. Maybe what one of us could brush off, the other carried and turned inward. The same environment, but two different stories being written beneath the surface.

And that's the part that feels both unsettling and important to name: we cannot perfectly control what our children take in or how they make sense of it. What we can do is widen the margin of safety—offering consistent messages, modeling neutrality and respect toward our own bodies, and staying curious when differences emerge instead of assuming sameness.

Because even in the same house, with the same people, children are not having the same experience.

And perhaps the goal was never to ensure identical outcomes, but to create enough safety, enough openness, and enough repair that each child has a chance to come back home to themselves, even if their paths there look very different.

Chapter Ten

Advocating for Your Child in a Weight-Focused Medical System

Having a child with developmental delays was one of the hardest and most isolating experiences I've had as a parent.

When Harris was born prematurely, we suddenly found ourselves dealing with physical therapy, occupational therapy, and speech therapy almost immediately. Everyone around me kept saying, "He'll catch up. He'll catch up." But all I could think was, "What if he doesn't? What do I do then?"

He did catch up, but not by accident. I gave everything I had to making sure he received every service and support available to him.

Olivia's hearing journey, however, was different. That is something that will be part of her life forever. In the beginning I remember thinking, "What do I even do with this? How do you put a hearing aid on a newborn?"

I quickly realized I would have to become an advocate for my children in ways I never expected. Harris had been premature, had a heart condition, and experienced speech delays. Olivia had hearing loss. None of these things made them fragile, but they did mean they had specific needs that required attention.

In those early months I remember thinking, "This shouldn't feel this hard. What is wrong with me? Why can't I handle this better?"

The truth is, becoming a parent often means stepping into situations you never imagined and learning how to navigate them in real time.

Unfortunately, medical environments can sometimes reinforce harmful messages. Pediatricians will often focus on correction, normalization, or milestones the child is "behind" on, with success being defined as becoming more "typical." Or they may ask children why they are overweight or what they are doing about it.

These moments can create shame in the child for bodily differences, and can lead to chronic self-monitoring, "Am I normal enough yet?" and difficulty feeling at home in their body. The message that often comes across is: "Your body is wrong, and here's how you should fix it."

Our culture reinforces this message: "if you don't like something about your body, get rid of it. Fix it. Change it." And sometimes those options do exist. But that doesn't mean they're necessary or you should use them.

As a parent advocating for your children, you can ask their pediatrician:

1. How can we make our wellness checks less focused on my child's weight?

2. Can you conduct a wellness check on my entire child, not just their weight?

3. What changes can they make?

We all want to protect and advocate for our kids. But we also have to be careful not to bubble-wrap them–something that can be hard to resist doing. Children still need exposure to the world. Completely shielding them from experiences, even uncomfortable ones, can limit opportunities to learn how to navigate difficult situations.

That doesn't mean you can't advocate for your child. There is nothing wrong with asking providers to be kind with their words, to stick to facts instead of opinions, and to be mindful of your child's developmental age.

The key is finding a middle ground between overprotecting your child and not advocating for them at all. Both extremes can be problematic. And of course, the age of your child will influence how involved you need to be.

Weight As an Indicator of Health

When many providers review a child's chart, one of the first questions asked is: "How much weight did they gain this year?" Although the medical field is slowly becoming more aware of the limitations of weight as a measure of health, it is still very often the first thing doctors look at.

But children are *supposed* to gain weight. They're growing. Their bodies are developing. Of course their weight is going to change. And yet many kids are still made to feel ashamed for gaining what someone else decides is "too much" weight.

Here's the thing, though, as I've mentioned a few times in this book before: Weight is not an indicator of health.

I repeat: Weight is not an indicator of health.

Our bodies are genetically predisposed to fall within certain ranges. More often than not, you will resemble some version of your parents or relatives unless something extreme alters that trajectory.

Even so, BMI (Body Mass Index) is regularly used as a screening tool to assess health, particularly for identifying potential weight-related issues. If the number is considered "too high" or "too low," then it becomes a concern.

Yet height is rarely treated the same way, even though height is largely determined by genetics, just like weight.

BMI is based on guidelines developed in the 1830s by Adolphe Quetelet. It was never intended to be used as a personal health tool. Quetelet created it as a statistical measure to describe the "average" body within a population, not to assess individual health (BMI Calculator, 2026). That didn't stop the World Health Organization from adopting BMI in 1997 as a tool to classify and treat obesity (Pray & Riskin, 2023).

It begs the question: How are we in 2026 and still relying so heavily on a measurement created nearly 200 years ago?

The world we live in today is drastically different from the one Quetelet studied. Our access to food, nutrition, medicine, and lifestyle options has changed enormously. It seems reasonable that we should have developed more accurate tools to assess health across diverse bodies by now.

BMI has long been criticized for its limitations and inaccuracies, especially when applied to individuals rather than large populations. It does not account for muscle mass, bone density, genetics, or the wide range of natural body diversity—particularly in women.

Pregnancy is a perfect example. At prenatal appointments, doctors weigh you—which makes sense medically. But according to the BMI scale, many pregnant women suddenly fall into the category of "morbidly obese," because of course they do. They are literally growing another human.

Similarly, professional athletes like swimmers or bodybuilders, who are in incredible physical condition, will fall into the overweight or even obese category according to this scale.

Even when these athletes have very low body fat, the BMI calculation can still label them as unhealthy simply because muscle weighs more than fat. If that doesn't tell you there is something wrong with using weight and BMI as a tool for assessing health, I don't know what does.

A perfect example of how fixated doctors can be on weight is the experience of one of my clients and her two daughters, one of whom struggles with overeating and the other with malnourishment because she's not eating enough.

Of course, when they got into the exam room, the doctor only focused on the child who was overeating, not the child whose body literally isn't working properly. He immediately launched into an interrogation of the younger girl: "Are you eating a lot of candy?" "How much exercise are you getting?" "You shouldn't be eating carbs."

My client, her mom, was so overwhelmed she couldn't even speak. She was frozen. All the way back to the car, the girl kept asking, "What's wrong with me? What's wrong with me? He made it sound like there's something wrong with my body."

No child should ever be made to think that there's something wrong with their body just because their pediatrician thinks they're overweight.

When it was the older daughter's turn to be examined, the doctor was dismissive at first of her mother's concerns of malnourishment, claiming that "three pounds wasn't that much to lose."

The girl wasn't underweight, but she was under-eating, and as we know–let's say it all together–weight is not a primary indicator of health. A number on a scale just doesn't give us enough information to make an assessment.

I advised my client strongly to push for bloodwork. If a person isn't getting the nutrients they need, they're more likely to be deficient in some important vitamins that are covered in a basic metabolic blood panel. Understandably, my client didn't realize that bloodwork could help determine whether her child was malnourished.

When I'm working as part of a treatment team—with a client, dietitian, psychiatrist, and physician—I'm not the one ordering labs. Typically, the dietitian will coordinate lab work through the physician. However, I am often the first professional a client sees. People rarely think to start with a dietitian or psychiatrist—they just know something feels off and reach out for therapy.

Because of this, I can help streamline the process by asking early questions like, "When was the last time you had bloodwork?" From there, we can decide whether it makes sense for them to request labs from their doctor or for me to connect them with a dietitian right away.

What can make this challenging is that bloodwork does not always tell the whole story. Sometimes labs come back within the normal range even when something serious is happening underneath. This is especially common with individuals who are purging. Electrolyte levels can appear stable at one moment and shift rapidly with repeated purging. Someone's labs might look normal, yet their body could still be at significant medical risk.

It's one of the reasons eating disorders can be so dangerous—they don't always show up clearly in the places we expect.

When Pediatricians Become the Weight Police

Pediatricians are trained within a medical model that often defaults to weight as the primary explanation for a wide range of problems. The message is frequently: Lose (or gain) weight first, and then we will consider what else might be going on.

This approach can lead to devastating outcomes, with the most obvious being missed or delayed medical diagnoses as well as disordered eating, body shame, and loss of the child's trust in their body.

Yes, life is easier if you're in a normative body, because people treat you nicer. As horrible as that is, that is the reality; that is the truth. But communicating that to a child, implicitly or otherwise, can be dangerous.

When children are vulnerable and looking to their parents and trusted adults for support and answers, this type of messaging can unintentionally become a first-class ticket to food restriction. That may not be the intention, but children interpret what adults say very literally. They trust us. And even if we explain that trying to change their body could harm them, they may still attempt to do it anyway.

It is so hard to be a parent and try to protect your kids from the world judging them based on their weight. Weight is such a small part of who they are.

I experienced weight judgment from a medical provider first-hand during a hospital visit with my three year-old, Olivia, while in the process of writing this book. The first thing they did when we got there was weigh and measure her. When Olivia stepped off the scale, the nurse immediately insisted the number wasn't right. She checked it four separate times, even had me get on the scale to "make sure it was working," before finally saying, "Wow, she really is 30 pounds."

I tried to stay neutral because the actual number doesn't matter to me. My child's weight makes no difference. What matters is if they are healthy and happy. But the nurse's preoccupation was so extreme that it was uncomfortable. If she had taken a moment to do the math or look at any growth-chart research, she would have known that the average three-year-old weighs 30 pounds (Miles, 2025).

Then the nurse added, "She doesn't look like she's 30 pounds. She must be so dense."

I was stunned. Dense? What did she mean by dense? It made me think of how people justify body differences by saying they have "big bones," even though bone size doesn't determine weight (Kennedy, 2021). It's just another way we rationalize our discomfort with bodies.

I was floored that she couldn't just take my child's weight for what it was. As a parent, it made me feel really uncomfortable. I understand that for surgery they need to know the patient's weight to determine how much medication to give, but that is really the only reason she needs to be weighed at the doctor's. Okay, maybe there are a few others, but that didn't change the nurse's reaction.

I was still bothered by it after Olivia's surgery. Part of it was thinking how if my daughter had been aware of what was going on, I would have reacted totally differently. If Olivia were eight years old, and they said, "That cannot be your weight," I would have responded with, "What are you saying? All bodies are different. What my child weighs has very little indication of how healthy she is."

I've heard from many clients how their medical providers respond to their kids' weight during their well-visits with their kids. Maybe the child is a little higher on the growth chart, or weighs a little closer to the skewed overweight guideline, prompting providers to make unhelpful comments, such as "What fruits and vegetables are you eating? How much are you moving?"

One of my favorite dietitian friends has a really great way of approaching this. She asks her clients, "What can you add to your meal plan? Can we add some fiber? Can we add some more green? Can we add some variety? Can we add a new fruit, a new veggie, or another form of protein?"

It's a very effective, non-judgmental way to involve the client in fueling their body with nutrients, without shaming them by saying, "Oh my God, you did not eat any fruits and vegetables this week!"

Instead, she approaches the conversation with curiosity and asks, "What are *you* willing to add to your meal plan?"

Interrogating a child or parent about what their child is eating or how they are moving does nothing to help move toward sustainable change. As a parent, you trust your pediatrician to do what is best for your kid. I would like to think the pediatrician does not *want* to shame your child into eating better, yet they say things like, "Wow, you have gained this much. That is a little bit more than we were hoping for."

This kind of doctor's visit can feel uncomfortable to the point where I have had to coach my clients through these conversations. I offer them a script to say to the doctor: "If you are going to talk about my child's food intake or their weight in a negative lens, I need you to allow them to go back to the waiting room so that we can talk about this."

Ideally, pediatrician appointments would be less focused on weight and more on well-being, wellness, happiness, and fulfillment. But if we as parents want that, we need to advocate for ourselves and our kids.

My client with the two daughters from the last section ended up meeting with her children's doctor to discuss his behavior, and since then he has been incredibly mindful of his word choices with both children. I would like to think he became equally mindful with his other patients as well. Imagine how many lives that could change, children's and parent's, on a practice level.

The Growth Chart

From birth to age 18, your development is followed on a growth chart. One can estimate how much you'll weigh as an adult based on how you have grown over the course of your childhood because our bodies want to stay on the curve.

Growth charts are one of the primary tools doctors, nurses, and pediatricians use to track development over time. They are a series of percentile curves that show how children grow (CDC, 2024). Every person has a natural growth pattern and weight range where their body functions best, and that natural well-weight can shift throughout our lives.

Growth charts use percentiles to track a child's development relative to other children of the same age and sex, and it is completely backwards. Doctors will say things like, "The kid is in the 98th percentile for weight, the 50th for height."

The 50th percentile is average, but Harris wasn't even on the freaking chart when he was born. That's how underweight he was. I remember the day that he got on the chart, we had this celebration moment. But basically, whatever we stay on in our percentage is usually how we will stay for life. If we naturally were in the 65th percentile when we were 13, we will likely stay there well into adulthood and old age. Consistent growth along an individual curve is often a reassuring sign of health.

Growth charts are very useful for tracking development and growth patterns, but they fail to account for genetic diversity, ethnicity, and normal variations in growth rates.

Many practitioners, myself included, feel that growth charts can cause unnecessary anxiety for parents, who often feel pressured to keep their child on a specific curve. Percentiles are frequently treated as goals rather than descriptions, but children grow in spurts and a shift in percentile doesn't always, or even usually, mean anything.

The growth chart can offer some valuable information, but it places too much emphasis on comparison between children whose bodies were never meant to grow in identical ways.

Empowering Your Child to Self-Advocate

One of the best ways to teach our children how to advocate for themselves is to model it. When you advocate for what matters to you, your children see what it looks like to stand up for yourself and protect your own mental health.

Self-advocacy is a life skill. Children practice advocating for themselves in school, but they learn it from us, their parents.

Before they ever learn to say "I don't like that," our children are watching how we respond to discomfort, boundaries, and pressure. They notice when we apologize for or set aside our needs, and if we say yes when we really mean no.

When we consistently override our own limits, our children learn that keeping other people comfortable is more important than listening to themselves. Eventually, this can lead to a disconnect from their own internal cues like hunger, fullness, and emotional overwhelm.

Your child needs to see you speaking up and engaging in a respectful dynamic with their doctor. In addition to modeling, this gives them tacit permission to speak up for themselves.

Because doctors are...well, *doctors,* many of us automatically trust their recommendations and follow their protocols without questioning them. We may even assume that everything they are doing or suggesting is required, when in reality some of their recommendations may be optional. Conversely, we may assume that they are doing all the necessary tests, asking all the necessary questions, and getting all the necessary information.

As parents, we need to get comfortable asking questions or challenging them if we don't understand or agree with something, or want more information.

I'm not suggesting that you approach your healthcare providers with skepticism. The majority of doctors and other providers are dedicated, educated professionals who want the best for your child. At the same time, it is important to remember that medical practitioners vary in their training and experience. Depending on their familiarity with eating disorders or malnutrition, certain tests may not automatically be considered.

Your child's healthcare provider should be one of the people you feel most comfortable talking to. They should be offering options and treating you like someone who has the ability to participate in decisions about your child's care.

Empowering your children to self-advocate requires helping them learn to express themselves, and listening when they do. As parents we are their training ground for communicating with adults and what to expect when they do.

In addition to modeling, here are some ways we can empower our kids to self-advocate:

1. Let them practice their voice. Many of us speak on behalf of our children out of love and efficiency. We answer questions on their behalf, order their food, even interpret their feelings for them. Instead, give them the opportunity to speak for themselves by gently turning the question back:

"Why don't you tell them?"

"What do you think?"

"Can you show me what you need?"

2. Teach them to listen before they speak. Self-advocacy begins with listening inward. Our kids can't advocate for hunger if they don't recognize hunger, or set boundaries if they can't identify and validate their own discomfort. Body trust and self-advocacy are deeply connected.

3. Help them learn to express their thoughts out loud. Encourage your child to proactively communicate (as opposed to simply answering questions) in a way that others can understand. Be patient when they express themselves awkwardly–they're learning! The goal is not to script their voice, but to help them discover it.

Ultimately, it's our responsibility as parents to advocate. If something feels off, ask questions and if it's appropriate, let your child see you addressing what is bothering you in a calm and constructive manner.

If you're still concerned about an eating disorder or nutritional deficiencies after speaking to your child's medical provider, request additional testing or consult with a licensed therapist who can help guide you on how to advocate for your child's care.

Key Takeaways

Becoming a parent often means stepping into situations you never imagined and learning how to navigate them in real time.

It's an unfortunate reality that medical environments can sometimes reinforce harmful messages. An overreliance on weight, percentiles, and growth charts often leads pediatricians to focus on correction, normalization, or perceived developmental gaps—defining success as becoming more "typical." In some cases, children may even be asked why they are overweight or what they are doing to change it.

These moments can create shame in the child for bodily differences, and can lead to chronic self-monitoring, "Am I normal enough yet?" and difficulty feeling at home in their body. The message that often comes across is: "Your body is wrong, and here's how you should fix it."

The default to weight as the primary explanation for a wide range of problems can lead to devastating outcomes, with the most obvious being missed or delayed medical diagnoses as well as disordered eating, body shame, and loss of the child's trust in their body.

For these reasons, it's imperative that we advocate for our child.

Self-advocacy is a life skill. One of the best ways to teach our children how to advocate for themselves is to model it. As parents we are their training ground for communicating with adults and what to expect when they do. Your child needs to see you speaking up and engaging in a respectful dynamic with their doctor. This gives them tacit permission to speak up for themselves as well.

Empowering your children to self-advocate requires helping them learn to express themselves, giving them the opportunity to practice their voice, and teaching them to listen inward. Our kids can't advocate for hunger if they don't recognize hunger, or set boundaries if they can't identify and validate their own discomfort. Body trust and self-advocacy are deeply connected.

We all want to protect and advocate for our kids. But we also have to be careful not to bubble-wrap them. Children still need exposure to the world, and shielding them too much from uncomfortable experiences can limit opportunities to learn how to navigate difficult situations.

The key is finding a middle ground between overprotecting your child and not advocating for them at all. Both extremes can be problematic. And of course, the age of your child will influence how involved you need to be.

Chapter Eleven

The Loaded Question: What is Health?

Health is not determined by any one thing, and it certainly isn't a number on a scale.

If you look up the dictionary definition of "health," it is often described simply as life without disease (Schramme, 2023). But even that definition is incredibly narrow, because so many different factors contribute to health.

Health is not "a look," nor is it just a number or a clothing size. It is something we are constantly working on and adjusting throughout our lives.

Physical health is only one piece of a much larger picture of well-being. True wellness also includes emotional, mental, social, and environmental health.

Think about it: How can someone expect their emotional or

mental health to thrive if they aren't addressing chronic illness, autoimmune conditions, or other medical needs? How can anyone feel well if they are only getting five hours of sleep each night or barely drinking water?

Health is built from many small, interconnected pieces working together.

Think about a disease like mononucleosis–or mono. The primary treatment is rest. The body needs time and basic support to recover. If we don't give our bodies their basic needs—enough food, enough sleep, enough water, and time for self-care—how can we expect anything else to function well?

Self-care, at its core, is about listening to your body and meeting its needs. Some people may define self-care as things like massages or spa days, and those things can be nice. But they are not the foundation.

If I'm not giving my body its most basic requirements—sleep, nourishment, hydration—how can I expect everything else to work?

I can't connect with my friends, work, or do things I enjoy if I'm completely depleted because I haven't eaten all day. I can't function well if I'm running on five hours of sleep and caffeine.

We often expect our bodies to perform like machines, but we forget that machines require fuel.

It's interesting when you consider how seriously people take the fuel they put in their cars, insisting on specific grades of gasoline for the best performance and engine protection. But when it comes to fueling their own body, that level of care is nowhere to be found.

Many people will make sure their children, even their pets, eat high-quality organic, farm-raised foods, yet they don't give themselves the same consideration. They feed themselves what's leftover, or what's available, or what's convenient.

But what if we lived a life guided by the idea that "this makes me happy" or "this is fun?"

Food should be exciting. It should be enjoyable. But too often exciting, enjoyable foods have been moralized and demonized, like we're supposed to sit there eating celery and rice cakes and pretend they're the most satisfying thing in the world.

We shouldn't have to pretend or restrict ourselves from eating foods we genuinely want—especially when we're sharing a meal with others and trying to connect with them. Food is meant to be social. It's meant to be part of living.

So the question becomes: How do we return to trusting ourselves?

Part of it is learning to make choices based on what actually feels right to us, instead of constantly thinking about what other people believe we should do. When we make decisions based solely on outside expectations, we slowly disconnect from who we really are and lose our sense of identity.

In my work with clients, I encourage them to start making choices that align with their own body, mind, and well-being. What feels nourishing? What feels fulfilling? What supports their mental and emotional health? That's how we begin rebuilding trust with ourselves.

It's similar to how we navigate other everyday choices. For example, I may still eat Chick-fil-A even though I don't agree with some of the views held by its leadership. Or I might shop at Hobby Lobby because I like certain things they sell, even though I don't agree with everything the company represents.

There are some things I draw a hard line on. But if something genuinely brings me joy or adds value to my life, I'm not going to deny myself that experience simply because someone else thinks I should.

Learning to trust yourself means allowing room for those decisions.

If we allowed every single person's opinion to dictate what we do, we wouldn't be able to go anywhere or do anything.

There will always be people who disagree with you—people who don't like what you believe, what you enjoy, or even who you are. Those differences exist everywhere.

At the end of the day, you have to trust yourself and the relationship you have with yourself. You have to allow space for your own ideas, opinions, and knowledge to develop. And at the same time, you can remain open to hearing other perspectives without fearing that simply listening will somehow change who you are.

Being open-minded doesn't mean abandoning yourself. It means being confident enough in who you are to engage with the world without losing your footing.

I once read an article about environmental health that argued one of the most important things we can give our children is a safe and stable environment (American Academy of Pediatrics, 2021). Psychologists often emphasize that children thrive when they have consistent, supportive relationships and environments where they feel secure and connected.

The article received a lot of backlash, though, because people pointed out something important: Not everyone has the ability to pick and choose their environment. Many families can only afford what they can afford. Housing, neighborhoods, schools—those things are often limited by circumstance.

But the truth is that stability does not only come from where you live. You can still create stability for your child through the values you build inside your home. A child can grow up feeling safe when there is honesty, connection, and a sense of belonging within their family. They can feel supported when they know they are part of a group that cares about them and shows up for them consistently.

Research shows that what protects children the most from stress is not necessarily perfect circumstances, but safe, stable, nurturing relationships with the adults in their lives (American Academy of Pediatrics, 2021). These relationships act as a buffer against toxic stress and help children build resilience over time.

In other words, the environment that matters most for a child is not always the zip code. It is the emotional climate of the home.

Feeling safe, loved, and connected is what allows children to grow, adapt, and navigate the world—even when life around them is imperfect.

Our environment plays a huge role in shaping how we live our lives. The reality is that we exist within many environments at once: our homes, our schools, our communities, our workplaces, and the groups we choose to be part of.

Because of that, it becomes even more important for our home to be the environment that feels the most stable. Ideally, it is a place where open-mindedness is encouraged, where everyone has a voice, and where thoughts and feelings matter.

While some environments may feel outside of our control, many actually are within our influence. For example, we can choose our religious environment if that is something important to us. We can choose the sports teams or activities we participate in. Those are environments we actively step into.

Schools can be more complicated. Sometimes families can choose between public or private schools, while other times they are limited by zoning or financial constraints. But even within those systems, there are still choices about what communities and activities we engage in.

In my own community, for example, people tend to lean on each other in meaningful ways. The Alamo Heights community is relatively small, and because of that, there is a strong sense of support. There are two elementary schools, one middle school, and one high school, and families often feel connected through those shared spaces.

Communities like that can become another layer of environment that helps children feel supported as they grow.

Community plays an important role in health. The social and environmental aspects of our lives often come together in ways that deeply influence our well-being.

Our emotional well-being and mental health are closely connected, but they are not just about our thoughts or belief systems. They are also about the way we speak to ourselves and how we build self-worth and confidence over time. For people of all ages, these things need to be intentional priorities.

Part of that includes developing what I would call healthy self-doubt—the ability to question ourselves in a way that helps us learn and grow, rather than immediately blaming or diminishing ourselves. Curiosity about our own thoughts and behaviors allows room for growth in ways harsh self-criticism never will.

Emotional health also requires awareness. We need to be able to recognize what we are feeling, express those emotions effectively, and build a coping toolkit that evolves as we move through life. What helped us regulate when we were five years old will probably not work when we are 35.

When children are young, their coping tools often look simple. Many have a favorite stuffed animal or blanket they rely on for comfort. I think about my son Harris, who had a lovey named Jeffrey that helped him regulate when he was little. As he has grown, he has needed it less and less. And that makes sense—I would not expect Harris to still rely on a lovey at 35 years old to regulate his emotions.

As we grow, our coping tools evolve. Physical comfort might come from a pet, a partner, a friend, or a hug from someone we trust. Emotional regulation becomes more complex than simply being told to "take a mindfulness breath." Breathing exercises can help, but real coping involves building a broader toolkit of support, connection, and self-understanding.

There is a difference between maladaptive coping mechanisms and adaptive coping mechanisms—the difference being whether the strategy actually helps you build a healthier quality of life.

A maladaptive coping strategy might be drinking alcohol to avoid feeling your emotions. It may work temporarily in the sense that it numbs the feeling, but it does not actually resolve anything. Over time it can become harmful or even addictive.

Adaptive coping strategies, on the other hand, are tools that help you process emotions and move through them. This might look like journaling, taking a walk to clear your mind, calling a friend, or taking a shower to reset your nervous system. None of these things magically fix your life, but they create space for you to process what you are feeling instead of avoiding it.

Emotional well-being and mental health are deeply connected, but most people are only taught how to express two emotions: happiness and anger. Those are the emotions that tend to be modeled and accepted in many environments.

But there are many more emotions than that. When people are not taught how to recognize or express them, they often end up suppressing what they feel or struggling to communicate it effectively. In some environments, emotions are not welcomed at all. People learn very early that certain feelings should stay hidden.

Part of emotional health is learning how to express those emotions in ways that can actually be heard. I often think of it like a volume knob. If you turn the volume all the way up and yell, people may stop listening. But if you turn the volume too far down, your voice disappears completely. The goal is finding the setting where you can be firm, clear, and heard.

Health can feel overwhelming because there are so many different pieces to it. But one helpful way to think about it is simply asking yourself: "Where are the gaps? Where are the areas in life where your needs are not being met?"

For example, if you are someone who thrives on social connection but you have not spent time with friends in months, that social part of your well-being may need attention. Sometimes improving health is not about fixing everything at once. It is about noticing where something is missing and taking one step toward filling that space.

TAKE ACTION

Grab your notebook again and take a moment to reflect. What is Health? To you? To the world? To your future?

When we talk about emotional well-being, a lot of people immediately feel lost. They think, "I don't even know what that means."

In session, I often ask a simple question: "What is the action urge that comes with fear?"

Many people cannot answer it. And if they cannot answer it, I teach it.

What does fear feel like on the inside? What does it look like on the outside?

Think about it this way: If a bear is running toward you, you are not going to think, *Let me go check that out.* Your body immediately shifts into fear. Your heart starts pounding. You sweat. Your body prepares to run.

That is the internal experience of fear.

But what about the external expression? How do we show fear on our face? How do we communicate it to others?

These are things we are rarely taught beyond early childhood. Maybe in pre-K someone showed us pictures of faces with different emotions. After that, many people never receive any education about identifying or expressing emotions.

And if you grow up in an environment where certain emotions are not allowed, you may never learn how to express them at all.

All of this connects back to health. Health is not a certain look. We know that people can hide a lot of what is happening inside their bodies. We cannot assume someone's health based on their appearance.

Sometimes physical changes can give clues—skin color, eye color, or other visible signs that something may be happening internally. But those are indicators, not guarantees. Just like the number on a scale or the size of someone's clothing is not a reliable measure of health.

Health is also not something we have to earn. Yes, our choices can influence our well-being. But health is ultimately about maintaining some level of stability, not about perfectly following a list of rules.

Many people are told how much sleep they should get, how much they should exercise, how much water they should drink, and how many meals they should eat in a day. Then they blindly follow those guidelines and feel like they have failed if they cannot check every box.

Instead, we have to learn how to listen to our own bodies. Your body may need more nutrients when you are more active, and fewer when you are less active. But that does not mean you should arbitrarily decide to go below a basic level of nourishment because you think that is what you are supposed to do.

Health is not about forcing your body into someone else's formula. It is about learning how to understand the signals your own body is giving you.

Approaching Health with Curiosity and Kindness

Our basic needs go beyond childhood. In fact, they never end.

Many people neglect their physical needs, even though meeting those needs can positively influence every other area of health. Part of the reason is that everyone wants a quick fix. But health does not work that way. It is not something that can be solved overnight.

Physical health often comes down to basic care: going to annual doctor's appointments, completing routine lab work, seeing the dentist, and generally taking care of your body. Yet once people age out of their pediatrician, many go years before establishing care with a primary physician.

Part of the work ahead of us is removing the shame and rigid expectations around health and replacing them with openness and curiosity about what health can look like. Success in health does not have to follow one narrow definition.

I never want someone to feel so much shame about their health that they avoid taking care of themselves altogether. It is never too late to begin again.

Instead, it can be helpful to ask simple questions: At this stage of my life, what could I do that might support my physical health? What choices would make me feel better in my body?

Approaching health with curiosity allows room for growth. When we shift away from shame and toward curiosity, we open the door to change instead of feeling stuck behind it.

Sometimes it can be helpful to ask questions within the different roles we play in our lives.

For example:

- Am I a better mom when I work out compared to when I don't?
- Do I feel stronger—physically and mentally—when I make time to build strength?
- Is my emotional well-being at work, at school, or at home

better when I prioritize sleep?

Questions like these allow us to notice how our habits affect the way we show up in our lives.

You could even think of this as a form of intellectual health—challenging your thoughts, learning new things, and questioning ideas simply because it is interesting to do so. When we allow ourselves to stay curious and ask better questions, we open the door to deeper understanding and new perspectives.

Alongside curiosity, there is kindness.

The most basic definition of kindness is the golden rule: treating others the way we would want to be treated. Kindness also includes giving people the benefit of the doubt and, at times, being willing to experience discomfort or make sacrifices for someone else without expecting anything in return.

This topic comes up often in my therapy sessions. When we do something for someone out of kindness, we have to ask ourselves an honest question: Is it actually kindness? Or are we expecting something in return?

If we are expecting praise, recognition, or repayment, then there is a good chance the action was not purely about kindness. Sometimes it is more about checking a box that reassures us that we are a good person.

Kindness also requires accepting that people are different. We all have quirks about ourselves that we love, and quirks about others that we appreciate. No two brains are exactly alike, which means we all perceive the world differently. Because of that, my idea of perfection will never be the same as yours.

So the real question becomes: How can we accept people as they are, rather than demanding that they adapt to our version of how things should be?

If everyone were the same, the world would be incredibly boring.

Kindness also has to extend inward. Being kind to yourself means interrupting that automatic self-critical voice when it shows up. Just as we would stand up for a friend who is being treated harshly, we need to learn how to do the same for ourselves. This is often the hardest part.

True kindness, toward others and toward ourselves, comes from choice. When we help someone, it is because we choose to, not because we feel forced to. When we offer support or make sacrifices, it is something we do freely.

And when those choices are freely made, the people we help do not owe us anything in return. We are simply responsible for our own decision to show up with kindness—for others, and for ourselves.

Kindness opened my eyes to how many different ways it can show up in our lives.

Kindness can look like being genuinely happy for someone else without focusing on the advantages they may have had. It can look like celebrating someone's success without resenting them for getting there first or having a different path. That, too, is kindness.

There are countless actions that fall under the umbrella of kindness, but the first step is letting go of the expectation that someone will notice or return it.

Think about something as simple as holding the door open for someone. If they walk through without saying thank you, does it irritate you? If it does, it is worth asking yourself an honest question: "Was I doing that out of kindness, or was I hoping for recognition?"

How often are our actions attempts to influence someone else's reaction? Are we hoping to earn praise, attention, or validation? Or are we simply acting in a way that reflects the person we want to be and the values we want to live by?

As I have gotten older, my relationship with giving back has changed a lot. I have found that I do not actually want attention for it anymore.

One Halloween, I made little jack-o'-lantern flashlights with each child's name on them for Olivia's classmates. My mom asked me afterward if the parents had said anything or if anyone had noticed. I told her no—because no one knew it was from me. For me, that was the point.

What matters now is trusting that what I choose to do is authentic. I have found the kinds of things that fill my cup and bring me joy. For me, that often looks like little holiday gestures or quiet acts of generosity. I do not need to be the "party mom" or the center of attention in a classroom. I just enjoy doing small things that feel meaningful. And that is something I have had to remind myself of often: Kindness and generosity will look different for every person.

After kindness comes change.

Change can feel more complicated because it requires awareness first. We have to notice that something in our life may need to shift. Then we have to decide whether making that change aligns with our values. And if it does, we have to figure out what the next step looks like.

The truth is that change is constant. Everything in life is always moving and evolving. If we refuse to move with it, we eventually find ourselves stuck.

In terms of mental health, change can actually open new possibilities. Simply being willing to try something different can create opportunities that did not exist before.

Life also becomes incredibly boring if we do everything the exact same way all the time. Predictability can feel safe, but eventually it becomes stagnant. Sometimes change happens because we learned a better way to do something. Sometimes it happens simply because trying something new is interesting.

We also tend to connect more easily with people who are flexible and willing to adapt. Rigid thinking makes relationships difficult, while openness to change signals trust.

In many ways, practicing change is like experimenting with life. It requires trusting that things will work out, even if the outcome is uncertain.

Being willing to change—or even to admit that we were wrong—is something we appreciate in other people because it requires vulnerability. When we allow ourselves to change, we allow others to see us as we really are: human.

Trying something new means risking imperfection. It means risking failure, embarrassment, or being seen in a different way. But it also means allowing ourselves to grow.

Change is inevitable. Everything in life is always shifting and evolving. If we refuse to adapt, we risk getting stuck in the past. And when we stay stuck in old patterns, we limit our ability to build the life we truly want. Ultimately, the life we want is only possible if we are willing to change.

Supplements & Nutrition

Let's be clear: We can get all the nutrients we need from food without having to take supplements. We really only need supplements if our body is deficient in a certain nutrient, and a supplement is the best option for treatment.

Vitamins and dietary supplements didn't grow to a $400 billion industry treating medically diagnosed nutrition deficiencies (James, 2025). Not only are many supplements not necessary, but you can actually get vitamin toxicity from taking them in excess (Wooltorton, 2003). So how many hundreds of dollars are you spending on food supplements that might actually be doing more harm than good?

There has been an increasing push for health supplements for kids from brands like Hiya (Hiya Health, 2024) which promotes daily use. While these products are often marketed as essential, most children do not need vitamin supplements if they are eating a reasonably balanced and varied diet, are growing well, and do not have medical conditions affecting absorption.

With so much misinformation in the food world, it is easy to get overwhelmed. Not to mention all the self-declared "experts" speaking on nutrition without proper credentials. An online nutritionist coaching certificate is not the same as a professional degree with hundreds of hours of schooling. Unfortunately, though, people will follow what these gurus and influencers say without question.

Never once has my pediatrician said, "Give your kids vitamins." Instead, he will ask me, "Do they have a balanced diet?" to which I usually respond with some version of "Yes, minus the vegetables."

To which he says, "Okay, cool."

I am finding time and time again that it takes more energy to sift through the misinformation and find facts than it should. Everyone has a different definition of what "healthy" looks like. There are so many food rules that parents have, that upon further investigation are based on a fear of being fat or gaining weight. Which as we now know is not an arbiter of wellness and good health.

If you or your child are not diagnosed with a nutritional deficiency and prescribed supplements by a medical professional, there is no reason to take them. Never take supplements just because they're being pushed by online health "experts" or medical influencers on your socials.

Eating Disorders

Part of the reason eating disorders are so common is that they can be hidden for a long time. Control is socially acceptable. People rarely question someone who says they are trying to "be healthier." It usually isn't until behaviors become extremely disordered that others begin to notice or ask questions.

What many people forget is that the majority of individuals with eating disorders live in what society considers a normative body. They don't necessarily look sick.

In fact, some of the most medically and psychologically ill individuals can appear perfectly healthy from the outside. Eating disorders are not limited to people who are visibly emaciated or extremely large. Because of that, the illness can remain hidden—and sometimes even reinforced.

When someone is praised for losing 20 pounds, the praise is directed at the outcome, not the path it took to get there. No one would knowingly congratulate someone for vomiting, abusing laxatives, or starving themselves for days at a time. But when the result is weight loss, the behavior behind it often goes unseen.

No one begins restricting food with the intention of developing an eating disorder. It usually starts with something much smaller: "I just want to lose a little weight," or "I just want to drop five pounds." But over time, these goals can spiral.

What begins as a small change can turn into something all-consuming. Suddenly the person cannot stop losing weight. Food, weight, and body size become the only things their brain focuses on. It becomes the only place they feel any sense of control or relief.

Disordered eating is often a direct result of overly controlling and restrictive diets that begin in childhood, even infanthood, imposed by parents with the best of intentions. Unfortunately, good intentions don't change the reality of the consequences.

Many times, the parents who impose the strictest rules around food are suffering from disordered eating themselves, and yes, it is usually related to the size, weight, and appearance of their bodies. Sometimes these habits and the messages surrounding them are so deeply ingrained, they are not even aware they have a problem. Eating disorder behaviors can be invisible. Fatness is not.

Many individuals with eating disorders experience co-occurring mood disorders, most commonly anxiety and depression. When someone's mood is severely impacted, their cognition can be affected as well. Decision-making becomes more difficult, and it can be harder to evaluate risks or make choices that support long-term well-being.

Cognition is particularly impacted when the body and brain are deprived of adequate nutrition. Brain functioning becomes compromised. Someone can be highly intelligent and still find themselves making decisions that are harmful to their health because their brain simply is not receiving the nutrients it needs to function properly.

This is one of the most difficult realities of treating eating disorders. The illness itself interferes with the person's ability to recognize the severity of what is happening.

In many cases, eating disorder behaviors overlap in what I refer to as the "trifecta"–the cycle of restriction, bingeing, and purging. This trifecta comes with the underlying mindset, "I restrict so I will not gain weight. I purge so I will not gain weight."

All eating disorders place enormous strain on the entire body. The digestive system, the brain, and other organs are put under significant stress when someone repeatedly cycles through restriction, bingeing, and purging.

It is important to state this clearly: You *can* be fat and healthy. That idea still feels impossible for many people to hold, but body size alone does not determine health. Someone in a larger body can be healthier than someone in a culturally "desirable" thin body.

Living in a larger body is not a moral failure. But the shame, restriction, and body surveillance children experience when they're taught that their bodies must be controlled at all costs—that's what causes the deepest wounds. That's what follows them for life.

And we wonder why so many people avoid eating disorder treatment! But the answer is not mysterious: they know it is often not safe to seek help. They know they may be shamed.

Anorexia

Anorexia Nervosa is an eating disorder marked by restriction—of food, of needs, and often of self. It can look like eating very little, avoiding certain foods, or following rigid rules around eating and exercise.

But underneath, it's not about discipline or "being healthy." It's often about trying to feel safe, in control, or enough in a world that feels overwhelming.

There are two primary ways this can show up:

1. Restricting Type

This is what most people think of when they hear anorexia—consistent restriction of food, rigid rules, and avoidance of eating. Control feels like safety, and eating can feel threatening.

2. Binge–Purge Type

This subtype includes periods of restriction, but also episodes of bingeing and/or purging (such as vomiting or misuse of laxatives). Even though it may look different on the outside, the same fear, control, and distress are driving it underneath.

There has been increasing discussion in recent years about the distinction between Anorexia Nervosa and what is currently labeled "atypical anorexia." Traditionally, Anorexia Nervosa is diagnosed when someone meets the psychological and behavioral criteria while also being significantly underweight.

However, many individuals experience the same intense fear of weight gain, body image distress, and restrictive behaviors without falling below a certain weight threshold. These cases are often diagnosed as atypical anorexia. Many clinicians and people living with the disorder find that label frustrating because the psychological experience and the behaviors involved are essentially the same.

Research suggests that atypical anorexia may occur two to three times more frequently than anorexia nervosa, especially among adolescents and young adults (Kramer, 2023). Because individuals with atypical anorexia do not appear underweight, the disorder is often missed, diagnosed later, or taken less seriously, even though the medical and psychological risks can be just as severe.

Regardless of body size, the illness is still centered on restriction and control. Individuals may severely limit food intake, engage in extreme dieting, fast for long periods, or exercise compulsively in pursuit of changing their bodies.

Over time, prolonged restriction can lead to malnutrition. When the body is deprived of the nutrients it needs, serious medical complications can occur, including loss of menstrual cycles, heart complications, bone density loss, and many other long-term health risks. Some of these consequences can even become permanent if not treated early.

Anorexia Nervosa, particularly when it involves significantly low body weight, has the highest mortality rate of any psychiatric disorder (Auger et al., 2021). Severe malnutrition affects the brain as well as the body. When the brain is deprived of adequate nutrition, cognition becomes impaired, emotional regulation becomes more difficult, and the risk of suicide and self-harm increases significantly.

In the binge–purge form of the illness, purging most commonly involves self-induced vomiting, though it can also include the misuse of laxatives or other methods meant to eliminate food from the body. When someone is deeply entrenched in an eating disorder, their thinking becomes heavily distorted. The brain is not processing information logically because it is malnourished and consumed by the pursuit of control.

Someone may feel lighter after vomiting and interpret that sensation as weight loss, even though what they are primarily losing is water and electrolytes. The body becomes dehydrated, but the belief that purging helps control weight can remain incredibly powerful.

Even when individuals are told repeatedly that vomiting or laxative use does not lead to meaningful or sustainable weight loss, the disorder often holds onto that belief. The individual's fear of gaining weight can override logical reasoning.

In some cases, people rely heavily on laxatives in an attempt to control their weight. Over time, chronic laxative misuse can cause severe damage to the digestive system. Sometimes the only way I can break through to a client about the seriousness of that behavior is by explaining the long-term risks, including the possibility of needing a colostomy bag if the colon stops functioning properly.

At its core, anorexia is often about control. For many individuals, restricting food or manipulating their body becomes a way to cope with feeling out of control in other parts of their lives. Unfortunately, once the behaviors take hold, the disorder can become powerful enough that stopping on one's own feels nearly impossible.

Bulimia

Bulimia Nervosa is an eating disorder that involves a cycle of eating and trying to "undo" that eating. A person may eat a large amount of food while feeling out of control, and then attempt to compensate—through vomiting, over-exercising, restricting, or other behaviors.

But underneath it isn't about food—it's about distress, shame, and a nervous system trying to find relief. The cycle often starts with restriction or rigid rules, which leads to a binge, followed by panic and attempts to get rid of it. Then comes guilt… and the cycle repeats.

There are two subtypes of bulimia:

1. Purging Type: This includes behaviors like self-induced vomiting or misuse of laxatives or diuretics to try to get rid of the food.

2. Non-Purging Type: Instead of vomiting or laxatives, someone may compensate through excessive exercise, fasting, or significant restriction after eating.

Both are bulimia. Both are serious. And both are driven by the same cycle of restriction, urgency, and relief-seeking.

Many individuals struggling with bulimia understand logically that these behaviors do not truly cause lasting weight loss. Purging primarily results in the loss of fluids and electrolytes rather than meaningful changes in body weight. But the physical and emotional discomfort of having a full stomach can feel extremely distressing.

Digestion begins as soon as food enters the body. The process starts in the mouth and continues through the esophagus, stomach, and intestines, where the body begins breaking down and absorbing nutrients and calories. Even if someone purges shortly after eating, the body has already begun this process.

Despite knowing this logically, the urge to purge can still feel overwhelming because the behavior is tied to the intense anxiety surrounding food and weight.

The medical risks associated with bulimia are significant. One of the most serious concerns is electrolyte imbalance caused by repeated bingeing and purging. Extreme vomiting can disrupt the body's electrolyte levels, which are essential for normal heart function. When these levels become unstable, it can lead to dangerous heart rhythm irregularities and, in severe cases, even heart attacks.

There are also many other physical complications. Repeated vomiting can cause tears in the esophagus, stomach ruptures, chronic acid reflux, and severe dental erosion as stomach acid repeatedly damages the enamel on the teeth. Once that enamel is lost, it cannot be restored (Hamura et al., 2014).

Living with bulimia places immense strain on the body. It is physically uncomfortable, medically dangerous, and often deeply distressing for the person experiencing it.

Individuals struggling with bulimia can become extremely skilled at hiding their behaviors. Repeated purging can become so practiced that vomiting may occur almost silently, allowing the behavior to remain hidden from others for long periods of time.

However, over time the physical consequences begin to appear. Dentists may notice significant enamel erosion and ask patients whether they have been vomiting regularly. Rather than seeking help, individuals deeply entrenched in bulimia sometimes avoid dental care altogether in order to avoid these conversations.

One common response after vomiting is immediately brushing the teeth. Unfortunately, this is one of the worst things someone can do. After vomiting, stomach acid coats the teeth, and brushing right away can spread the acid across the enamel and accelerate erosion. Toothpaste alone cannot neutralize the acid. Safer immediate steps include rinsing the mouth with water, a baking soda solution, or certain mouthwashes that help neutralize the acid before brushing later.

In my work with clients, there are times when a harm-reduction approach becomes necessary. When someone is still actively struggling with bulimia, the immediate goal is not always complete cessation of the behavior, but reducing the damage it causes while working toward recovery. That can mean teaching clients small steps to protect their bodies—such as how to minimize dental damage or reduce other medical risks—while we continue addressing the deeper issues driving the eating disorder.

Part of being a therapist is helping people work their way out of these patterns, but it doesn't happen overnight. You can’t simply tell someone who has been purging five times a day for two years to stop and expect that to work. They often cannot stop immediately, even if part of them truly wants to, which is when I would utilize the Harm-Reduction Model.

The idea behind harm reduction is to slowly reduce the damage being done, one step at a time. So, instead of asking, "Can you stop this behavior right now?" the question becomes, "If this behavior is happening, how can we make it as safe as possible while we work toward change?"

With bulimia and purging behaviors, that might mean focusing on practical steps first. For example: How can someone get electrolytes into their body after purging? Can they try to eat something small afterward to help stabilize their system? How can they protect their teeth from further damage? Can they commit to getting regular lab work so we can monitor what is happening inside their body?

By breaking the process into smaller, achievable pieces, the work becomes more manageable. Each step reduces harm while building momentum toward recovery. Over time, these small changes can add up until the purging behaviors are no longer a part of their life.

The differences between anorexia and bulimia can sometimes be confusing. There can be overlap in behaviors, and some individuals may move between these diagnoses over time. Even so, each disorder has its own defining patterns.

Binge Eating Disorder (BED)

Binge Eating Disorder is defined by recurrent binge-eating episodes. A binge episode has two core features:

- Eating in a discrete period of time (often described as within about two hours), an amount of food that is definitely larger than most people would eat in similar circumstances.

- A sense of loss of control during the episode (feeling unable to stop or regulate what or how much one is eating).

Binge episodes are typically associated with several additional markers. These can include eating much more rapidly than normal, eating until uncomfortably full, eating when not physically hungry, eating alone because of embarrassment, and feeling disgusted, depressed, or very guilty afterward with a marked distress, occurring on average at least once a week for three months and not regularly followed by compensatory behaviors (like purging), or occurring exclusively during anorexia or bulimia.

Many people assume Anorexia Nervosa is the most common eating disorder, but binge eating disorder is widely described as the most common—and it is also frequently under-recognized and under-treated, in part because of weight stigma and the misconception that bingeing is simply a "lack of willpower."

When someone is in the midst of a binge, they may eat quickly, past the level of comfort, and without physical hunger. Many people binge in private because shame and embarrassment can be so intense. And even during the episode—or immediately afterward—people often report waves of guilt, shame, and disgust.

There is a particular cruelty in how BED is stigmatized. People with BED are often mislabeled as lazy, undisciplined, or "gross," when what they are actually experiencing is a serious mental health condition that deserves competent, compassionate care.

A common misconception is that people who binge "just need to stop eating." But many individuals with BED can eat a balanced meal and feel satisfied—then later still feel pulled toward a binge. Often, bingeing functions as an attempt to regulate emotion, numb pain, or cope with distress. It can feel like relief in the moment, even though it is usually followed by heavy shame.

Treatment is most effective when the goal is not weight loss, but rather addressing the behavior, the function, and the triggers. What sets the urge in motion? What does the binge temporarily solve? What skills can help someone ride out the urge without acting on it? Evidence-based approaches (including eating-disorder-focused psychotherapy such as CBT-based treatments) focus on reducing binge episodes and improving the relationship with food—not on shrinking the body as the primary outcome.

It's also important to be honest about outcomes. In any eating disorder recovery, bodies may maintain weight, lose weight, or gain weight. We cannot ethically promise a body outcome. What treatment *can* aim for is the reduction of disordered behaviors, greater psychological flexibility, and a more stable, nourished life.

A key diagnostic distinction with BED is that it does not include recurrent compensatory behaviors (like self-induced vomiting or excessive exercise to compensate). If compensatory behaviors are present, the diagnosis may shift (for example, toward bulimia nervosa), and diagnoses sometimes need to be updated over time as symptoms change.

And here is a truth worth saying plainly: BED can occur in people of all body sizes. Body size is not a diagnostic criterion, and eating disorders do not discriminate. They affect people across genders, racial and ethnic groups, ages, and socio-economic backgrounds.

This also means access to competent care is not evenly distributed. Stereotypes about what an eating disorder "looks like," along with disparities in access to specialty treatment, contribute to many people being missed, dismissed, or treated too late.

The Role of Fatphobia

Many people—consciously or unconsciously—hold the belief that individuals in larger bodies do not deserve help. At the same time, there is widespread confusion about the fact that someone can be in a larger body and not have binge eating disorder at all. These nuances are still deeply misunderstood.

One client shared with me that her father had always been extremely fatphobic. At one point, he told her that one of the reasons her parents divorced was because her mother had "gotten fat," and growing up, she often heard comments like, "Don't end up like your mom."

His comments didn't come out of nowhere. They came from a culture saturated with fatphobia. Confronting those messages takes ongoing work, and many of my clients struggle with intense internalized fatphobia even while actively receiving eating disorder treatment.

Because binge eating disorder does not lead to immediate, dramatic medical crises in the same way anorexia or bulimia can, it is often taken less seriously. Anorexia carries a high risk of death from cardiac complications. Bulimia can result in severe electrolyte imbalances due to purging. Binge eating disorder, by contrast, is quieter—and its consequences are frequently minimized or overlooked.

Of the three most commonly known eating disorders, binge eating disorder, bulimia, and anorexia, I would say that binge eating disorder is the least researched. Anorexia Nervosa was formally recognized in the 1970s. Bulimia nervosa followed in the 1980s. Binge eating disorder was not officially recognized until the early 2000s and remains under-diagnosed, under-treated, and under-researched, in large part because many people in larger bodies avoid seeking care out of fear of shame, judgment, and dismissal.

Night Eating Syndrome

Night Eating Syndrome (NES) occurs when individuals consume the majority of their food in the evening or binge at night. This pattern is often the result of inadequate nourishment earlier in the day. Many people are attempting to restrict, to "be good," or to control their intake—but by nighttime, biological hunger catches up.

Once home, with access to food and fewer external constraints, the body responds to deprivation with urgency. These episodes are not about lack of discipline; they are the predictable outcome of restriction followed by unmet physiological need.

When the body is consistently denied food during the day, it will eventually demand it—loudly.

Night Eating Syndrome vs. Binge Eating Disorder

Night Eating Syndrome (NES) and Binge Eating Disorder (BED) are often confused, but they are not the same condition, though they can overlap.

Night Eating Syndrome is characterized by a pattern of eating that is shifted later into the day. People with NES often consume about 25% of their daily intake in the evening or during the night (Kabir & Salman, 2022). This may include waking from sleep to eat and then returning to sleep. Importantly, these episodes are not always experienced as a loss of control. Instead, they are often driven by prolonged daytime restriction, disrupted hunger cues, stress, or circadian rhythm dysregulation.

Binge Eating Disorder, on the other hand, involves episodes of eating an objectively large amount of food in a discrete period of time with a clear sense of loss of control. Binges are often rapid, secretive, and followed by intense shame, guilt, or disgust. While restriction can absolutely contribute to binge eating, BED is also strongly linked to emotional regulation, trauma, and learned coping patterns.

To help distinguish between the two disorders, an accurate assessment is needed, not simplistic, harmful advice like "Just stop eating at night."

Neither disorder is about willpower. Both are about unmet needs. When we stop moralizing eating behaviors and start listening—to hunger, stress, safety, and satisfaction—we can begin addressing the root causes rather than blaming the symptoms.

Recovery & Relapse

People often respond to disordered eating by saying, "Well, if it's a problem, just stop." But if it were that simple, eating disorder treatment centers would not exist. Recovery is not something you can simply turn on and off.

It is similar to how many people assume obsessive-compulsive disorder (OCD) is just someone washing their hands repeatedly, when in fact it is far more complex than that—it's a neurological disorder that affects how the brain processes thoughts and behaviors.

Eating disorders function in a similar way. They become deeply wired patterns that are extremely difficult to interrupt.

Recovery is possible for many people, but it requires both willingness and an incredible amount of work. It is rarely quick or easy. It involves facing painful emotions, rebuilding relationships with food and the body, and learning entirely new ways to cope.

Even after someone reaches recovery, the work does not simply end. Maintenance becomes part of the process for the rest of their life. Understanding that reality is important, because recovery is not about perfection. It is about continuing to return to the work, again and again, when life inevitably shifts.

Research shows that relapse is common, with estimates suggesting that anywhere from 20–50% of individuals with eating disorders experience some form of relapse during recovery in the first year (Setliff, 2025).

That doesn't mean treatment didn't work—it means recovery is not linear.

It's important to note that relapse in eating disorder recovery does not mean failure—it means something in the system needs more support, attention, or care. These patterns are deeply wired, and returning to old behaviors is often part of the process, not the end of it.

The truth is that relapse rarely comes out of nowhere. More often, things have been building for a while. Someone may have been experiencing increased stress, major life changes, depression, anxiety, or other vulnerabilities that were not being addressed or prioritized.

What matters most is not avoiding relapse entirely, but how quickly it's recognized and supported. Recovery isn't defined by perfection. It's defined by the ability to return, repair, and keep going.

In many cases, relapse is less about the triggers and more about returning to familiar coping behaviors during difficult moments. These behaviors do not disappear completely just because someone enters recovery. They remain part of the brain's learned response patterns. What changes over time is a person's ability to recognize those urges and choose a different response.

Recovery is not about eliminating those thoughts entirely. It is about becoming more skilled at noticing them and deciding not to act on them because you understand they don't lead you toward the life or goals you truly want.

Our brains are excellent at storing old coping strategies. Even when they feel far away, those patterns are still there and they can start to look appealing again, especially during stressful times. The brain might try to bring these strategies back with a very convincing message: "Remember when this worked for you? Maybe you should go back to that."

But that voice is misleading. It is offering a false sense of control.

A big part of relapse prevention is learning to recognize the early warning signs. Sometimes it's something as simple (and honest) as noticing a thought like, "Wow, I'm really liking that I lost five pounds because I had the flu for two weeks."

That thought might pop up unexpectedly, but a thought is just a thought. It doesn't mean you have to act on it. The question then becomes: "What can I do to protect myself instead of engaging in behaviors that follow that thought?"

This is where relapse prevention plans become important. For people who are still in therapy, this might mean talking through vulnerabilities and creating strategies together. For someone who has not seen their therapist in a while, it might mean reaching back out and having a conversation about what is currently feeling difficult.

Relapse prevention plans are essential because relapse often grows in silence. Many people do not talk openly about the possibility of relapse with friends or family. Eating disorder behaviors can be hidden easily, and for some people the secrecy itself can become part of the pull.

Every relapse prevention plan will look different because everyone's vulnerabilities are different. For one person, a breakup might completely destabilize them, especially if their partner had been a major support in their recovery. Maybe that partner helped plan meals, encouraged regular eating, or helped keep recovery a priority. Without that support, the person may suddenly realize they never learned how to maintain recovery on their own.

For the college students I work with who are in recovery, midterms and finals are particularly vulnerable periods. Stress increases, routines change, and time becomes scarce. Without planning ahead, those moments can easily become relapse points.

Knowing this, many of them build protective strategies in advance. Some will meal-prep before exam week. Others will pick up extra work shifts so they have money to order food when they are too overwhelmed to cook. Some will go home for the week so their parents can help with meals instead of staying alone in their apartment.

Those kinds of preparations may seem small, but they can make a significant difference in protecting recovery during vulnerable moments.

Ways to Break the Stigma of Eating Disorders

1. Talk about eating disorders more openly. Normalize conversations so people don't feel alone, ashamed, or "too much" to share.

2. Educate yourself. Learn what eating disorders actually are (not stereotypes) so you can better understand and support your child.

3. Find local and online resources. Know where to turn for treatment, referrals, or support—for yourself or a loved one.

4. Challenge harmful comments in real time. Speak up when you hear diet talk, body shaming, or misinformation.

5. Stop labeling bodies as "good" or "bad." Shift away from moralizing food and body size.

6. Use person-first, compassionate language. Avoid defining someone by their disorder—see the whole person.

7. Share accurate information on social media. Use your platform (big or small) to spread awareness and truth.

8. Support those who are struggling without trying to "fix" them. Listen, validate, and encourage professional support when appropriate.

9. Acknowledge that eating disorders don't have one "look." They affect people of all sizes, genders, ages, and backgrounds.

10: Model a healthy relationship with food and your body. The way you talk about yourself matters—to others more than you think.

11. Encourage early intervention. The sooner support is sought, the better the outcomes.

12. Support organizations and advocacy efforts. Donate, attend events, or share resources that expand access to care.

Mental Health Protections in Your State

I am a member of the International Association of Eating Disorder Professionals (iaedp™). Our San Antonio chapter was founded in 2019, and I have been involved since the very beginning.

During my time serving as president of the chapter, I created an event called Recovery with Our Community. The goal of the event was to bring together eating disorder treatment providers and community members in a way that felt welcoming and supportive rather than clinical or intimidating.

Treatment programs and recovery resources at the event host interactive tables where attendees can participate in activities like cookie decorating, flower bouquet making, bracelet making, and other hands-on experiences. At the same time, the providers are able to share information about the services they offer and how they support individuals struggling with eating disorders.

In my work, I see how isolating this experience can feel. Many people believe they are the only ones going through it. But the truth is that entire communities of professionals and peers exist to support recovery. They don't need to do it alone.

I created Recovery with Our Community because of my deep

commitment to connecting people with resources. Whether someone is struggling with an eating disorder themselves, supporting a loved one, or navigating recovery, access to information and community support can make an enormous difference.

Unfortunately, there is still a tremendous amount of shame surrounding eating disorders and eating habits in our society. Because of that stigma, many people do not realize what resources exist around them, or feel too afraid to seek them out.

Even when events are designed specifically to offer support and information, attendance can remain relatively small. It's not that people do not need support. The shame and stigma surrounding eating disorders can make it incredibly difficult for people to show up publicly, even when the goal is simply to learn about the help that is available.

The reality is, there are more resources available than most people realize. Therapists, community groups, support networks, and advocacy organizations all exist to support individuals and families navigating eating disorders or disordered eating.

Insurance and Eating Disorders

You may have more access to care than you think. Many states have laws that require insurance companies to cover mental health treatment—including eating disorder care—on par with physical health services. This can mean that therapy, nutrition counseling, and other services are covered, even when people assume they aren't.

Unfortunately, many families never explore these options because they believe treatment will be too expensive or too difficult to access. But sometimes, simply understanding what your state requires insurance companies to cover can open doors people didn't know existed.

Treatment for eating disorders may include therapy, residential care, in-patient treatment, or partial hospitalization. Even in these programs, a single day in a 10-hour treatment program, without insurance, can cost at least $1,200. For a minimum of six weeks, the costs can quickly become unaffordable. Unfortunately, not everyone has the ability to pay for that level of care.

Sadly, insurance coverage for eating disorders is severely lacking in most of the country. The insurance industry fails everyone, but it particularly fails those struggling with eating disorders. It often involves a process where individuals have to "fail" a certain number of times before insurance will actually approve the time needed for proper care to get someone to a more stable place. Then, once the individual finally gets to the place they need and gets the help they deserve, they are discharged and work their way back to being monitored in outpatient care. The problem is, being discharged from a high level of care does not mean someone is fully recovered. Insurance companies typically focus on weight restoration or basic medical stability when determining discharge, but true recovery goes far beyond those markers.

In many ways, post-discharge is when the real work begins. Continued support, therapy, and structure are often needed even more during this phase. Recovery does not happen the moment someone becomes medically stable, and an immediate step-down without adequate support can leave individuals vulnerable to relapse.

Part of the recovery journey includes integrating back into everyday life without engaging in disordered behaviors. Unfortunately though, insurance rarely provides coverage for support throughout the recovery process.

Finding a Credentialed and Trusted Provider

If you needed heart surgery, you would not go to a general surgeon—you would go to a cardiologist or a cardiac surgeon who specializes in that area.

The same idea applies when seeking treatment for something specific like an eating disorder. Training in eating disorder treatment is not typically included in standard therapist education. It simply is not part of the general training protocol.

Everything I have learned about treating eating disorders has come through additional education that I chose to pursue and invest in on my own. I did that because I wanted to be the best clinician I could be for the clients I work with.

When you are searching for a provider, seeing credentials that indicate someone specializes in eating disorders can provide reassurance. Those letters after someone's name often signal that they have pursued additional training beyond basic education.

That does not mean a provider without a specific credential cannot be helpful. But it is reasonable—and important—to ask questions about their experience and training.

For example, you might ask:

- What program did you complete for eating disorder training?
- How long did that training take?
- Did you receive supervision hours as part of it?

These kinds of questions help you understand whether the person treating you has the knowledge and experience needed to support you effectively.

It takes significant time and commitment to gain specialized training in eating disorder treatment. That is why it can be difficult when someone shares that they “treat eating disorders,” but their training consists of attending a two-day conference.

It can feel jarring when a weekend workshop is equated with the thousands of hours of training, supervision, and direct clinical experience that many specialists invest in this work.

That said, I cannot say with complete certainty that a therapist without a specific credential is not capable or not effective. There are certainly skilled clinicians who have gained meaningful experience in other ways.

Access to treatment, however, is a different story. Not everyone who needs help is able to receive it because of financial barriers, insurance limitations, or lack of specialized providers. Parents are encouraged to seek out alternative resources through community-based organizations, government-funded programs, school-based services, and non-profit support organizations.

Key Takeaways

Health isn't something we arrive at, it's something we stay in relationship with. It shifts with our life, our needs, our seasons. There will be times we feel aligned and grounded, and times we feel disconnected or unsure. The same applies to our children.

When we listen instead of forcing, approach with curiosity instead of judgment, and model caring for our body not because we want it to look a certain way, but because it carries us through life.

If our basic needs aren't being met—sleep, nourishment, hydration—nothing else holds. We can't think clearly, connect with people, or show up fully when our body is depleted.

Food is part of that, but not as something to control or moralize as many of us have been taught. When we start making choices based on what actually feels good in our body, instead of what we think we "should" do, that's where trust begins to rebuild.

Disordered eating and eating disorders can develop at any age and are influenced by a range of factors. While overly controlling or restrictive feeding practices in childhood can increase risk, they are not the sole cause. In some cases, parents who enforce strict food rules may be navigating their own complicated relationships with food or body image. Even when intentions are protective, these dynamics can shape how a child begins to relate to food, their body, and internal cues over time.

Eating disorders become deeply wired patterns that are extremely difficult to interrupt.

Many individuals with eating disorders experience co-occurring mood disorders, most commonly anxiety and depression. Cognition is significantly impacted when the body and brain are deprived of adequate nutrition. Decision-making becomes more difficult, and individuals may find themselves making choices that are harmful to their health.

This is one of the most difficult realities of treating eating disorders. The illness itself interferes with the person's ability to recognize the severity of what is happening.

Recovery is possible for many people, but it requires both willingness and an incredible amount of work. It is rarely quick or easy. It involves facing painful emotions, rebuilding relationships with food and the body, and learning entirely new ways to cope.

Even after someone reaches recovery, the work does not simply end. Maintenance becomes part of the process, potentially for the rest of their life. Understanding that reality matters, because recovery is not about perfection. It's about coming back to the work, again and again.

Unfortunately, there is still a tremendous amount of shame surrounding eating disorders and eating habits in our society. Because of that stigma, many people do not realize what resources exist around them, or feel too afraid to seek them out.

The reality is, there are more resources available than most people realize. Therapists, community groups, support networks, and advocacy organizations all exist to support individuals and families navigating eating disorders or disordered eating.

When searching for a medical provider, it's important to find someone you trust to support your needs. Seeing credentials that indicate a specialization in eating disorders can offer reassurance—such as working with a Certified Eating Disorder Specialist (CEDS), which reflects additional training and expertise beyond basic education.

That said, a provider without a specific credential can still be helpful. What matters most is their experience, training, and ability to provide informed, compassionate care. It is both reasonable and important to ask questions so you can make an informed decision.

For example, you might ask about the type of eating disorder training they have completed, how long that training lasted, and whether it included supervised clinical hours. These questions can help you better understand whether the provider has the knowledge and experience to support you effectively.

Final Words

At the end of all of this, there isn't a perfect way to raise a child.

There is only a "present" one.

One that listens more than it corrects.One that gets curious instead of controlling.One that makes space for a child to feel, to hunger, to change, to grow, without rushing in to fix what was never broken.

You will not get it right every time. None of us do.There will be moments you fall back into what you were taught.Moments you question if you're doing enough, or doing it "right."

But this was never about getting it right.

It was always about the relationship.

If your child learns that their voice matters, that their body can be trusted, and that they are safe to be seen as they are, you have given them something far more lasting than any rule, plan, or perfect response.

You have given them a place to return to within themselves.

A place that says: I can listen. I can trust. I can stay.

And long after they stop asking what you think, long after they begin making their own choices, that internal voice will remain.

Not because you controlled it.But because you protected it.

You trusted the listener.And in doing so, you taught them how to trust themselves.

About the Author

Becca Allen, LPC, NCC, CEDS, PMH-C, is a highly respected Licensed Professional Counselor known for her expertise in eating disorders, personality disorders, perinatal mood disorders, and treatment-resistant mental health conditions.

As the founder of Becca Allen Counseling, PLLC, she brings a compassionate, research-driven approach to her work with individuals, families, and couples in San Antonio.

Becca earned her Master of Science in Clinical and Mental Health Counseling from the University of Texas at San Antonio. A strong advocate for evidence-based practice, Becca specializes in Dialectical Behavior Therapy (DBT) and Radically Open Dialectical Behavior Therapy (RO DBT).

In 2019, Becca earned her Certified Eating Disorders Specialist (CEDS) designation from the International Association of Eating Disorders Professionals (iaedp™). Becca is one of the founding members of the San Antonio chapter of the iaedp™, which launched in 2019.

The mission of iaedp™ is to promote education, training, and a standard of excellence among professionals who treat individuals with eating disorders. Becca has held board roles including Treasurer, Hospitality Chair, President, and Vice President, and is currently serving as Treasurer for the second time.

During her time as President, she created and developed San Antonio's first Recovery with Our Community to promote local resources for eating disorder treatment and to highlight the work of San Antonio-area providers.

Becca is committed to staying at the forefront of mental health treatment, consistently integrating the latest research and best practices into her work.

When she's not in the office, you can find her enjoying early morning Pilates classes, spending time with her husband and children, or fully embracing her favorite granny hobbies.

Works Cited

American Academy of Pediatrics. (2021, August 1). *Preventing Childhood Toxic Stress: Partnering With Families and Communities to Promote Relational Health.* American Academy of Pediatrics. https://publications.aap.org/pediatrics/article/148/2/e2021052582/179805/Preventing-Childhood-Toxic-Stress-Partnering-With?autologincheck=redirected

Auger, N., Potter, B. J., Ukah, U. V., Low, N., Israël, M., Steiger, H., Healy-Profitós, J., & Paradis, G. (2021, September 9). Anorexia nervosa and the long-term risk of mortality in women. *World psychiatry : official journal of the World Psychiatric Association (WPA), 20*(3), 448–449. https://doi.org/10.1002/wps.20904

Baskin, A. (Writer and Director), Dunlop, S. (Writer), French, K. (Writer), Cullen, C. (Director), Ross, D. (Writer and Director), Stewart, G. (Director), Gallagher, T. (Director), Rupel, D. (Director), Cohen, A. (Director), Pridey, J. (Writer). (2013, November 4). Season 4 (Season 4, Episode 1) [TV series episode]. In A. Hoegl, B. Bernstein, L. Shannon, P. Healy, & A. Cohen (Executive Producers), *The Real Housewives of Beverly Hills.* Evolution Media.

Baswick, J. (2024, February 12). *Clean plate club: What it is & how to leave*. The Intuitive Nutritionist. https://theintuitivenutritionist.com/clean-plate-club/

Ben-Joseph, E. P. (Ed.). (2019, August). *Growth charts | Nemours KidsHealth*. KidsHealth. https://kidshealth.org/en/parents/growth-charts.html

Best Beginnings - creators of Baby Buddy. (2023, April 5). *Signs Your Baby Is Hungry*. YouTube. https://youtu.be/xNEU2buSwls?si=IVS1k2R5XKCgxwwe

BMI Calculator. (2026, February). The Complete History of BMI: From Quetelet to Modern Medicine (1832-2026). BMI Calculator. https://www.calculatemybmi.net/blog/bmi-history/

Boyle, J., Contis, D., Foley, S., Garfinkle, D., Morton, J., Rankin, S., Renfroe, J., Story, D. (Executive Producers). (2013–present). *Naked and afraid* [TV series]. Discovery Channel.

Centers for Disease Control and Prevention. (2024, September 2). *Growth charts*. Centers for Disease Control and Prevention. http://www.cdc.gov/growthcharts/index.htm

Chrisler, J., & McHugh, M. (n.d.). *Fat Shaming in the Doctor's Office Can Be Mentally and Physically Harmful*. American Psychological Association. https://www.apa.org/news/press/releases/2017/08/fat-shaming

Cleveland Clinic. (2022, October 17). *Relaxin: Hormone, production in pregnancy & function*. https://my.clevelandclinic.org/health/body/24305-relaxin

Colgate. (2024, August 30). *Preventing baby bottle syndrome.* Colgate. https://www.colgate.com/en-us/oral-health/kids-oral-care/preventing-baby-bottle-syndrome

Combination feeding and maintaining milk supply. WIC Breastfeeding Support - U.S. Department of Agriculture. (n.d.). https://wicbreastfeeding.fns.usda.gov/combination-feeding-and-maintaining-milk-supply

Fontana, L. (1592). *Venus and Cupid* [Painting]. Musée des Beaux-Arts, Rouen, France. https://mbarouen.fr/en/oeuvres/venus-and-cupid

Festinger, L. (1954). A theory of social comparison processes. *Human Relations, 7*(2), 117–140. https://journals.sagepub.com/doi/10.1177/001872675400700202

Gale, M. (2020, October 6). *Satiety: How does it work?*. Sugar Nutrition Resource Centre. https://www.sugarnutritionresource.org/news-articles/satiety-how-does-it-work

Giel, K. E., Thiel, A., Teufel, M., Mayer, J., & Zipfel, S. (2010, March 4). Weight bias in work settings - a qualitative review. *Obesity Facts*, *3*(1), 33–40. https://doi.org/10.1159/000276992

Hiya Health: Essential super nutrients for kids. Hiya Health | Essential Super Nutrients for Kids. (2024). https://hiyahealth.com/

Hunger and fullness awareness | Johns Hopkins Medicine. (n. d.). https://www.hopkinsmedicine.org/health/wellness-and-prevention/hunger-and-fullness-awareness

James, S. (2025. November 25). Dietary Supplements Market to Hit $414.5B by 2033, Growing at 8.9% CAGR - Key Trends & Insights by Grand View Research, Inc. *PR Newswire.* https://www.prnewswire.com/news-releases/dietary-supplements-market-to-hit-414-5b-by-2033--growing-at-8-9-cagr--key-tre nds--insights-by-grand-view-research-inc-302625579.html

Kabir, R. & Salman, E.J. (2022, September 14). Night Eating Syndrome. *National Library of Medicine.* https://www.ncbi.nlm.nih.gov/sites/books/NBK585047/

Katella, K. (2021, June 15). Eating Disorders on the Rise. *Yale Medicine.* https://www.yalemedicine.org/news/eating-disorders-pandemic

Kennedy, S. (2021, August 18). *Big-boned, big myth*. Motion Health & Fitness. https://motionhealth.net/2021/08/18/big-boned-big-myth/

Kramer R. (2023, February 16). Considerations in Evidence-Based Treatment of Adolescents With Atypical Anorexia Nervosa. *Journal of health service psychology*, *49*(1), 41–51. https://doi.org/10.1007/s42843-023-00080-1

Massey, R. J., Moon, R., & Ackland, T. R. (2023). Weight variability and cardiovascular outcomes: A systematic review and meta-analysis. *Cardiovascular Diabetology, 22*, 1–17. https://doi.org/10.1186/s12933-022-01735-x

Michel, A. (2025, August 8). *Weight stigma and food bias*. The Emily Program. https://emilyprogram.com/blog/weight-stigma-and-food-bias/

Miles, K. (2025, April 29). *What's the average height and weight for babies and toddlers – and does it actually mean anything?* BabyCenter. http://www.babycenter.com/baby/baby-development/average-weight-and-growth-chart-for-babies-toddlers-and-beyo_10357633

Mishra, S., Beshai, S., Feeney, J., Fogg, C., & Iskric, A. (2026). Perceived disadvantage: Individual differences in sensitivity to unfavorable social comparison predict poorer mental health. *Personality and Individual Differences, 255*, 113677. https://www.sciencedirect.com/science/article/abs/pii/S0191886926000401

Newborns have small stomachs. Newborns Have Small Stomachs | La Leche League Canada. (n.d.). http://www.lllc.ca/newborns-have-small-stomachs

Niewijk, G. (2025, March 6). *Do kids need milk?*. UChicago Medicine. http://www.uchicagomedicine.org/forefront/pediatrics-articles/do-kids-need-milk

Ochner, C. N., Tsai, A. G., Kushner, R. F., & Wadden, T. A. (2019). Physiological and epigenetic features of "yo-yo dieting" and weight cycling. *Current Diabetes Reports, 19*(12), 139. https://doi.org/10.1007/s11892-019-1273-4

Otsu, M., Hamura, A., Ishikawa, Y., Karibe, H., Ichijyo, T., & Yoshinaga, Y. (2014, November 19). Factors affecting the dental erosion severity of patients with eating disorders. *BioPsychoSocial medicine*, *8*, 25. https://doi.org/10.1186/1751-0759-8-25

Pascarelli, E. (Director). (2023). *Not Just a Picky Eater* [Film]. Pascarelli Productions.

Peebles, R., Muhlheim, L., & Sumner, B. (2024). *A weight-inclusive approach for calculating estimated target weights for adolescents* [Conference workshop]. International Conference on Eating Disorders. https://www.aedweb.org/aed-events/iced-2024/iced-20

24-workshop-summary-session-1

Phelan, S. M., Burgess, D. J., Yeazel, M. W., Hellerstedt, W. L., Griffin, J. M., & van Ryn, M. (2015). Impact of weight bias and stigma on quality of care and outcomes for patients with obesity. *Obesity Reviews*, *16*(4), 319–326. https://doi.org/10.1111/obr.12266

Pray, R., & Riskin, S. (2023, November 3). The History and Faults of the Body Mass Index and Where to Look Next: A Literature Review. *Cureus*, *15*(11), e48230. https://doi.org/10.7759/cureus.48230

Renew Bariatrics. (2024, January 12). *Weight Loss Industry Statistics: How Big is the Market.* Renew Bariatrics. https://renewbariatrics.com/weight-loss-industry-statistics/

Rhee, E. J. (2017). Weight cycling and its cardiometabolic impact. *Journal of Obesity & Metabolic Syndrome, 26*(4), 237–242. https://doi.org/10.7570/jomes.2017.26.4.237

Robbins, M., Rinaldi, K., Brochu, P. M., & Mensinger, J. (2025). Words are heavy: Weight-related terminology preferences are associated with larger-bodied people's health behaviors and beliefs. *Body Image*. https://www.sciencedirect.com/science/article/pii/S1740144525000117

Roth, G. (1991). *When food is love: Exploring the relationship between eating and intimacy*. Penguin Books.

Schramme, T. (2023, July 22). Health as Complete Well-Being: The WHO Definition and Beyond. *Public health ethics*, *16*(3), 210–218. https://doi.org/10.1093/phe/phad017

Setliff, S. (2025, September 15). *Eating Disorder Relapse Is Com-*

mon: Here's Why and What to Do About It. Eating Disorder Center. https://www.eatingrecoverycenter.com/resources/eating-disorder-relapse-statistics

Society for Endocrinology. (n.d.). *Relaxin: Hormones*. You & Your Hormones. http://www.yourhormones.info/hormones/relaxin/

Tribole, E. (2018). *What is intuitive eating?*. Intuitive Eating. http://www.intuitiveeating.org/what-is-intuitive-eating-tribole/

UAB Medicine. (2022, March 7). *MyPlate Healthy Eating Chart Replaced the Food Pyramid*. UAB Medicine. https://www.uabmedicine.org/news/myplate-healthy-eating-chart-replaced-the-food-pyramid/

Waking up hungry: Night eating syndrome. Cleveland Clinic. (2025, November 7). https://my.clevelandclinic.org/health/diseases/21731-night-eating-syndrome-nes

Watson, S. (2024, September 26). *Understanding your hunger cues and intuitive eating*. A Little Nutrition - Winnipeg Nutrition Dietitian + Therapy Services. http://www.alittlenutrition.com/understanding-your-hunger-cues-and-intuitive-eating/

Wegovy comes with significant health risks. Physicians Committee for Responsible Medicine. (n.d.). http://www.pcrm.org/news/blog/wegovy-comes-significant-health-risks

Weight loss medication: Wegovy® (SEMAGLUTIDE) injection 2.4 mg. Weight Loss Medication | Wegovy® (semaglutide) Injection 2.4 mg. (n.d.). http://www.wegovy.com/.

Wooltorton, E. (2003, July 8). *Too much of a good thing? toxic effects of vitamin and mineral supplements*. CMAJ : Canadian Medical Association journal = journal de l'Association medicale canadienne. https://pmc.ncbi.nlm.nih.gov/articles/PMC164945/

Worobey, J., & Worobey, H. S. (2014). Body-size stigmatization by preschool girls: In a doll's world, it is good to be "Barbie." *Body Image, 11*(2), 171–174. https://doi.org/10.1016/j.bodyim.2013.12.001

Zou, H., Yin, P., Liu, L., Liu, W., Zhang, Z., Yang, Y., & Liu, J. (2019). Body-weight fluctuation was associated with increased risk for cardiovascular disease, all-cause and cardiovascular mortality: A systematic review and meta-analysis. *Frontiers in Endocrinology, 10*, 728. https://doi.org/10.3389/fendo.2019.00728

www.ingramcontent.com/pod-product-compliance
Ingram Content Group UK Ltd.
Pitfield, Milton Keynes, MK11 3LW, UK
UKHW062308290726
14090UKWH00018B/955

9 781961 826144